JOURNEY

OF

DISCOVERY

TO

PORT PHILLIP,

NEW SOUTH WALES;

BY

W. H. HOVELL,

AND

HAMILTON HUME:

IN

1824 and 1825.

Printed on acid free ANSI archival quality paper.
ISBN: 978-1-78139-283-6
Photo by DAVID ILIFF. License: CC-BY-SA 3.0

Contents

DEDICATION

TO SIR THOMAS BRISBANE, BART. K.C.B.

In testimony of respect for his military conduct, and scientific acquirements; of esteem for his upright and honorable Administration of this Government; (his enlightened endeavours to introduce amongst us the free Institutions of the Mother Country; and especially his patronage of a Free Press, that most precious of all boons to this distant land:) as well as of attachment for his many amiable qualities and private virtues--this publication, whose objects are intimately connected with the interests of a Colony, in which his name and merits will ever be revered, and his memory gratefully cherished, is inscribed by his very obliged and faithful and obedient servant,

W. Bland.

Sydney, New South Wales.

PREFACE

An explanation is due for the lateness of this Publication, and it is therefore necessary to state the Gentlemen who performed the journey, were at first, (a circumstance often connected with real merit) fearful that their exertions were hardly deserving of public notice; nor were they induced to change this opinion, until a considerable time after their return,--nor then, but at the suggestion of their friends. This circumstance was some time afterwards mentioned to the Editor, who with much pleasure undertook the arrangement of the papers, but was prevented in the commencement of his task by an illness, which did not allow him to resume his design for many months, when, a considerable portion of the work having been actually printed, a new and most unexpected obstacle to its progress occurred, it being announced that *the printer* had no more paper, and that it was utterly impossible at that time to procure a supply of that article in the Colony.

The late journey of Captain Sturt down the Murrambidgee, which may be considered a mere continuation of the previous plan of Messrs. Hovell and Hume, it is hoped will be admitted a happy opportunity for their present, though late introduction of the results of their laborious undertaking to the public, not only on account of the important intrinsic value of their labors, but from their almost inseparable connection with those of the latter traveller. Thus to give a geometrical idea of the relation of the route of Messrs. Hume and Hovell, and of that of Captain Sturt, it may be said, that the line of march of the former may be considered as the base line of a triangle, one side of which is formed by the route of Captain Sturt, the other by the line of coast to the southward, extending from Encounter Bay (in which is situate the Emboucheur of the Lake Alexandrina[1]), to Port Phillip: and the whole contents of which triangle, a space of about 112,500 square miles, consisting generally of an extremely fine country, intersected by numerous streams and rivers, are now by the conjoint labours of Messrs. Hovell and Hume, and of Capt. Sturt, laid open to the public.

The real merit of the task of the two original travellers will be best estimated by a reference to the work of the late Mr. Oxley, Surveyor General, in which the very FINE country actually TRAVERSED by them is denounced as[2] UNINHABITABLE, and according to the prevailing opinions of that time IMPASSABLE also; indeed, the Colonists must well remember how hopeless the attempt of these two travellers appeared at the time at which it was undertaken. However, by their courage and perseverance, and almost without assistance, the work was achieved, and by it an accession of information respecting the interior of this country acquired, far superior to any thing that had preceded it, and which, as far as regards this Colony, cannot indeed hereafter be readily surpassed.

The object of the Editor, which had been completed at the time when the publication was discontinued from the want of paper, was to embody in his detail all the more valuable facts, and remarks which were to be found in the journals of the two travellers, preserving as nearly as possible their own method of description, and risking now and then the chance of becoming tedious to the general reader, for the sake of giving such precise topical information as he conceived would enable any one, who was so inclined, to follow their track, or such as would be interesting and important, if not indispensable, to persons, who might feel disposed to settle in those Districts, which he describes. His little leisure from professional pursuits he regrets, left it not in his power to do much more; and with this explanation he ven-

---

[1] See Appendix, No. 3.
[2] We had DEMONSTRATED BEYOND A DOUBT, that no River could fall into the Sea, between Cape Otway, and Spencer's Gulf, at least none deriving its waters from the Eastern Coast, and that the Country South of the parallel of 34, and West of the Meridian 147, 30 East, was uninhabitable and useless for all the purposes of civilised man.
Oxley's Journal, APPENDIX--Page 372.
See also Pages 74, 80,100,101, and 106, of the same journal, in which the same opinion is still more positively and strongly expressed.

tures to submit the work to the kind and considerate indulgence of the reader.

In the Appendix will be found the narratives of the two journies of Captain Sturt,[3] as published in the *Sydney Gazette,* of dates April 9, 1829, and May 13, 1830, and which, with the description of Western Port, and its vicinities, extracted from the narrative of a journey performed by Mr. Hovell[4], will it is hoped, form a body of information (the greater part of which has never before been presented to the public) respecting the interior of this country, not only highly creditable to the enterprising individuals by whom the several journies were performed, but of much interest both to the Colonists, and to the civilised world at large.

An error which occurred in the original title page of this work is to be explained, in which the name "Port Phillip" ought to have been, and is now, substituted for Western Port, and whence it appears, that the travellers had, from the imperfection of their instruments injured as they were in the journey, as well as from the hurried manner in which some of their observations were unavoidably taken, committed an error of about thirty or forty miles in longitude, an error that it is hoped, will readily be pardoned, and which was not detected, so little of the country was at that time known, but by Mr. Hovell's subsequent journey to Western Port, (see appendix.)[5]

Respecting the description of Western Port and its vicinities one remark which I beg now to submit, will place the importance of that document and of other similar documents in their just point of view, namely, that it has been the want of such information as they alone are calculated to supply which has caused so many settlements to be established, always at vast expense to the public, and often to the utter ruin of individuals, and which yet have scarcely been formed, ere it has become indispensable to abandon[6] them. But the value of such labours

---

[3] No. 4.

[4] No. 5.

[5] No 6.

[6] E. G. Port Phillip which was settled many years ago, and abandoned, as it will appear from this very Journal, from a mere want of a knowledge of the numerous advantages it possessed, and of later years Melville Island, Port Raffles, with Port Essington, not to mention the disappointments, the anxieties and the miseries experienced in the present attempt to settle Swan River,

need not be insisted upon with those who are in want of that information which they alone can afford. With the Colonists, of a young extending Colony, like that of New South Wales, and with the British public, who have from a thousand causes, so deep, and daily extending an interest in its welfare, and advancement.

The names given by Messrs. Hovell and Hume to plants and other Botanical productions met with in their journey are here retained; no specimens of plants having been collected by those Gentlemen, from which alone their more precise denominations could have been ascertained. The Geological specimens produced, were examined, and named by Mr. Alexander Berry, of Sydney.

Some extracts from a letter[7] addressed in the year 1826, to Colonel Dumaresq will explain the opinions of Messrs. Hovell and Hume at that time, and will testify the sound judgement by which they were guided in their laborious investigations as well as in their views for making future discoveries.

I will now only add, that the value of the labors of Messrs. Hovell and Hume is becoming daily more and more developed to the Colonists in the already extensive and extending occupations of land in those regions first introduced to the knowledge of the Public through their exertions, not to mention the late journey itself of Captain Sturt which as to the principles on which it was conducted, originated with those travellers while from the personal information of Mr. Hume during his accompaniment of Captain Sturt, in his previous excursion down the Macquarie and Darling rivers, the leading information and hints for his latter enterprise were almost solely derived.

Since writing the above, it has been thought advisable to add two or three papers to the Appendix, as well as to subjoin here a few remarks relative to those papers, and to the present state of the Colony as a point of immigration.

---

and the result of which enterprise is yet quite uncertain.--Port Jackson too itself, may be mentioned as another instance of the effects to form Settlements without a due degree of the necessary local information; settled as it was by mere accident, and in consequence of the well known disappointment, that was met with in the original attempt to settle on the shores of New Holland.

[7] Appendix, No. 6.

The Paper, No. 7, the Colonial Petition, now on its way to England, has been signed by 3525 free inhabitants, and among these signatures are the names of nearly the whole of our most respectable Colonists. The motives for this Petition were not only the conviction of the utter unfitness of the existing form of Government for the present state of the Colony--but they were the result of the repeated endeavours of the Colonial Government to wrest from the Colonists the only possible check upon their Rulers, "a free Press." *This* created the first alarm among the Colonists, who plainly perceived, that should the Government prove successful in this one point--not only would they remain subject to the most oppressive form of Government in the known world, but that they would be thus placed without any practicable appeal whatever for redress. Our Courts, however well known and often proved, the integrity of the present Colonial Bench, are scarcely any protection--and would, could the Government have succeeded in this fatal measure, (and which there was at one time too much ground to expect) have soon ceased to be any at all, under the present system, in which the Prosecutor has been known to appoint his own Jury, and therefore it may not be unfair to say, has been allowed to decide his own cause, and eventually to continue to inflict or remit in his own pleasure, the awarded punishment. It is to obviate this state of things that the Colonial Petition is now submitted to the Home Government.

The Paper, No. 9, is the Prospectus of a kind of High School, on an extensive scale, for the Education of our Youth. The land for this Institution was given so long ago as the year 1825, by Sir Thomas Brisbane. The Prospectus of this Establishment contains every information relative to itself, that can be required. I have only to add, that it has had many and considerable difficulties hitherto to encounter, and hence the tardiness of it's progress: but which although slow, is becoming every day more and more certain;--and there is every reason to hope that it will not be long ere this most important of all Institutions will be in active and beneficial operation.

With a School, such as the one proposed, and in which the appointment of Masters and the admission of Pupils, will rest with the numerous body of Proprietors, and with that amendment in the system of our Colonial Government, which the Petition points out,--the scope of fine country made known to the Public in the present publication, may be considered a happy Asylum for the surplus population of the Mother Country. But without a better form of Government, a confirmed "*Free Press*," and Institutions for the Education of Youth, it would be in vain to look to these shores as a refuge--where an increase of population would become an increase of evils, tending eventually, unless obviated, by some such means as those proposed for adoption, to estrangement from the Mother Country (a circumstance to be equally deprecated by both parties) to distress and anarchy.

The Paper, No. 8, is a copious extract by permission from the Report of the President of our Agricultural Society, and which will prove highly interesting to those who are desirous of information on the subjects of which it treats.

I shall merely in brief observe here, that the Colony of New South Wales is admirably adapted to the production of the Olive, and the Vine, and that there is every reason to believe it is capable of affording at all times, ample supplies of every description of grain for its own consumption--that it abounds in excellent timber, and that its present staple exports are wool, whale oil, seal skins, and woods, and that, in addition, it is commencing to export largely the following articles, viz.--hides, tallow, New Zealand flax, and spars, the extract of Mimosa bark for tanning, and various other minor productions.

It has manufactories for hats, coarse woollen cloths, and blankets, leather, salt, soap and candles;--it has also several breweries, and two distilleries in the vicinity of Sydney, both admirably situated, and on a scale of magnitude fully adequate to all the wants of the Colony--with four steam mills, exclusive of numerous water mills and windmills, employed in manufacturing flour--and finally an internal revenue of about £100,000[8], and a population of not less than 60,000 inhabitants, according to the most authentic accounts, though not in conformity with the last official census; but which for various reasons, it is concluded cannot be correct.

I shall conclude these prefaratory remarks, with one observation, which from its high interest I have expressly reserved for that purpose, namely, that it would be a matter of the greatest importance to the Emigrant, that the Government should devise some means by which

---

[8] EXTRACTED FROM THE COLONISTS WITHOUT THEIR CONSENT; AND OF THE APPLICATION OF WHICH THE LOCAL GOVERNMENT NEITHER RENDERS NOR SEEMS EVEN TO CONSIDER ITSELF BOUND TO RENDER ANY ACCOUNT TO THE PUBLIC!!!

the Emigrant might, on his arrival on these shores, be put in the earliest possible possession of his land. Delay in this respect being always highly injurious, and but too frequently equivalent to ruin. The plan that I would propose for this purpose is--1st. That the Emigrant should be furnished, without unnecessary delay, with the Government Order for his land *here,* in conformity to, or in ratification of, an order, with which he ought to be provided from Home on his embarkation, on his having shown here that he had fulfilled the conditions of such order-- namely, that he had brought with him such property or monies as had been stipulated--agreeably to the schedule produced by him, at *Home,* with the allowance of such deductions as might be *considered proper* by the Home Government, for the expenses of his outfit, passage and freight. 2dly. That a monthly corrected chart should be kept at the Surveyor General's Office in Sydney, always open for public inspection, so that the Emigrant in selecting land, might not commit the too frequent mistake of selecting such as had been already appropriated--after repeated fruitless, but expensive and harassing journies in search of his proposed allotment, and which under the present system of conducting this Department, there is no possible way for him to avoid. Copies of these corrected charts should also be kept at the various Districts at which the different Surveyors reside--and, 3rdly. That preference of grants, should be given to priority of choice, as evidenced by official lists, corrected daily and equally with the charts, accessible by the public. Better plans than the above may be suggested. It however appears infinitely preferable to the one at present in use, and should it do no more than bring this very important subject under the serious consideration of the Authorities, it cannot fail altogether of its proposed utility.

Sydney, New South Wales, January 10, 1831.

JOURNEY OF DISCOVERY
TO
PORT PHILLIP

Saturday, October 2, 1824.--Messrs. Hovell and Hume having met, as it lay in their route, at Mr. Hume's house, commenced their journey from Appin, in the County of Cumberland, accompanied by six men[9], a couple of carts, containing their supplies, drawn by four bullocks, and two horses, having also one spare horse, and a spare bullock; and each of the men as well as themselves, provided either with a musket or fowling-piece. At seven, they halt for the night, opposite to a point of land called Bird's-eye corner, on the Cowpasture, or Nepean, River.

Sunday, Oct. 3.--At nine in the forenoon they ford the river, but not without much difficulty, from the steepness and loose sandy nature of the banks, as well as from the heavy lading of the carts. Here they commence measuring with the perambulator, and having travelled three miles halt for the night near some waterholes, adjoining the boundary line of Mr. D'Arietta's fine Estate. The weather fine, but hot for the time of year.

Monday, October 4.--Renew their journey, proceeding along the road that leads into Argyleshire.[10]

---

[9] Appendix No. 1.

[10] The road was at this time, little more than a mere track. A more perfect road has been since contracted, forming the great Southern road into the interior.

The result of their measurements were as follows:--The place of their departure in the morning to Carriage-creek, seven miles and a quarter; this to the Stone-quarry-creek two miles and a half, and this again to Klensendorlffe's Inn, (where they remain the night,) three miles and a half, thirty rods. The entire distance travelled this day, being sixteen miles and a quarter.

Tuesday, October 5.--Leave Klensendorlffe's, cross the Bargo-river, and thence proceed, to Meehan's forest, where they remain the night. The distance travelled to-day, fourteen miles and a half.

Wednesday, October 6.--Arrive at the watering place in the Mittigong range, by ten o'clock in the forenoon; here halt. The weather sultry. At two in the afternoon, again move forward; cross the Bong-Bong river by five o'clock, and rest on its banks for the night. The distance from Meehan's forest to Mittigong, seven miles and a half, thence to the river, six and a half; the total distance travelled to-day, fourteen miles.

Thursday, October 7.--Had not proceeded more than five miles, when, the carts requiring some repairs, they availed themselves of the assistance of a blacksmith living in the neighbourhood for that purpose, and stop during this short detention at the house of Mr. James Atkinson, with whom they breakfast. In the evening pass through Wombat brush[11], and arrive a little before sunset at Patrick's River; here halt for the night. The distance from Bong-Bong River, to Wombat brush ten miles, thence to Patrick's river four and a quarter. The total distance from Bird's eye corner sixty two miles.

Friday, October 8.--Continue their route along the same road as hitherto, and reach Boombarloo (a distance of eight miles) before breakfast. Here they remain three hours, then proceed seven miles to Mr. Barber's farm. The distance travelled to-day, fifteen miles.

Saturday, October 9.--This spot offering plenty of feed for the cattle, which appear fatigued, they are allowed to rest. Mr. Hovell proceeds to Dr. Reid's and Lieutenant Futter's farms (both in the

---

[11] This brush, like most other parts of the country frequented by the animal from which it takes its name, is an excellent light soil. Not so the country through which they passed about Patrick's river; than which nothing can be worse.

neighbourhood,) and remains the night at the house of the latter gentleman.

The weather fine during the earlier part of the day; towards evening, some appearances of rain.

Sunday, October 10.--Mr. Hovell goes to Dr. Reid's house, and thence to Mr. Surveyor Harper's tent, at Jocqua, that he may compare their own compasses with those of Mr. Harper. On his return finds Mr. Hume and Mr. Barber, at Dr. Reid's house. The latter part of the day cloudy and attended with rain; and during the night heavy and continued rain, accompanied at intervals with squalls from the eastward.

Monday, October 11.--Resume their route, cross a tract of poor country, (part of Cookbundoon range,) and at dusk reach the carts, waiting for them at the waterholes under the Governor's hill.[12] Here they remain the night. Weather squally, with rain from the eastward. The distance from Mr. Barber's, through the range, is twenty-one miles. Road not good.

Tuesday, October 12--Cross the plains in the direction W. by S W. to Broughton's stockyards; thence continue their progress W S W. to the third Breadalbane Plains. Here they halt, at the distance of seventeen miles from the place (the Governor's hill) at which they had slept the preceding night[13].

Wednesday, October 13.--Arrive at Mr. Hume's station[14], about one in the afternoon, having travelled this day, eight miles and a half,

---

[12] These fine fertile plains or downs, are now well known to the colonists, and there is consequently, required no description of them here. At about fifteen miles N E. of these downs there is a considerable quantity of very fine marble of various colours.

[13] Here they turn off the track or bush road along which they had hitherto been travelling.

[14] The land, many miles around Mr. Hume's station, it extremely good; the hills thickly timbered, the low lands more scantily. The trees consist of different kinds of the gum; and among these of a peculiar species called the manna tree (eucalyptus mannifera.) This, in general appearance, is not much unlike the box, and produces large quantities of a white sweetish substance, somewhat resembling manna (whence its name) and which falls from it during the winter in large quantities, a little after sunrise.

W S W. Total distance from Bird's eye corner, one hundred and twenty three miles and a half.

Thursday, October 14.--Messrs. Hume and Hovell, with two of the men, proceed to Lake George, in order to ascertain the bearings and distance of the Lake from Mr. Hume's station. The latitude of which is, by account, 34 48 S. and by double altitude, 34 51. The longitude by account 149 21 E.

They arrive on the borders of the Lake, about 11 in the forenoon. The Lake bears S. 26 E. and is distant from Mr. Hume's station about twelve miles. They obtain a fine view of the lake from one of the lofty hills on its banks. This Lake is about twenty miles in length, in breadth about eight, inclosed almost entirely with thickly wooded steep hills; and which towards the South are surmounted by lofty mountains. The soil in the neighbourhood of the Lake is in general excellent, except on the hills[15]. They return at dusk; the weather unsettled.

Friday, October 15.--Squalls at intervals, but with little rain. The day occupied in writing letters, and in preparations for to-morrow's journey.

Saturday, Oct. 16.--Weather cloudy, towards evening, threatening rain. Prevented from renewing their journey to-day, by the unexpected desertion of a native guide, who had promised to conduct them through a part of the country, in their advance.

---

[15] It is said that the natives will not taste of the waters of the lake. Yet those travellers who drink of it, do not perceive any thing disagreeable either in the taste or otherwise. There is a story among the natives, that Lake Bathurst, a piece of water situate about ten or twelve miles to the eastward of Lake George, (and which is between three and four miles long, but somewhat less in breadth) has been entirely formed within their own time; and that they re-member the site which it occupies being dry land. It has evidently become much increased in size within the last eight years. It was discovered, as well as the surrounding country, by Mr. Surveyor Meehan and Mr. Hume, in 1817, when, from the scantiness of our information of the interior, more particularly in the immediate vicinity of the settlements, a discovery, even of this trivial extent, was not unimportant. To these gentlemen the Colony is indebted also for the first knowledge of Goulburn Plains, and of nearly the whole of the country in this direction. A species of pine is discovered on some of the high-est mountains south of Lake George; the wood of which promises to be highly useful.

Sunday, October 17.--Leave Mr. Hume's station (the last which is settled or occupied by the colonists) without a guide; travel twelve miles S. 60 W. (through a country affording good pasturage for cattle, thinly wooded and well watered) then rest for the night. The soil, near the spot where they halt, is composed principally of coarse schistus and granite.

Monday, October 18.--They start about seven this morning, their route lying across an extensive range of hills, S. This range which is of moderate elevation, lies between their last station and Yarrh. In crossing this range they marked the trees, in the course of their route, with an axe. The range itself, extending in the directions N W. and by N. and S E. and by S. consists of poor land but thickly wooded. About noon Mr. Hovel ascended an elevation on the top of the range, at a little distance on the right hand of their route, which they named "Mount Lookout." From this hill there is a pleasing view of the country[16] in their advance, consisting of plains skirted by fine extensive forest, and this bounded to the Southward by mountains. A little after noon, they begin to descend the south side of the range towards Yarrh, through a country almost the exact counterpart of that which they had just passed in their ascent. Soon after descending the range, they ford a small stream, the Gondorroo, a branch of the Murrumbidgee; along which stream they travel one or two miles and then halt. The plains seemed here to be extensive, and formed a fine sight, the soil good, consisting of vegetable decompositions, and the disintegrations of granite and limestone[17], large masses of both of which descriptions of rock were seen here and there, lying on the surface. The plains too were interspersed with occasional clumps of the Native Honeysuckle, sure indications of a loose, light, good soil. The average direction of their route, S. 45, W.; distance, travelled, eleven miles.

Mount Look-out bears from the place (the last marked tree,) at which they entered the plains, N E. by N. and is distant about six miles.

---

[16] Yarr. These plains they afterwards named "M'Dougall Plains," from the family name of Lady Brisbane.
[17] Considerable quantities of shells, embedded in limestone, were discovered in various parts of these plains.

Another high forest mount which stands by itself, W. 60, N. distant about ten miles, they named after his Excellency the late Governor, "Mount Brisbane."

Tuesday, Oct. 19.--Resume their journey; pursuing the direction[18] S W. by W. half W.; and having travelled about two miles and a half, arrive at the highest spot of land in the plains. This is nearly due S. of Mount Brisbane, and distant from it about ten miles.

Yarrh, Yass, or M'Dougall's Plains, extending in the directions N W. and S E. consist for the most part, of clear land generally level. The soil dry and good. These plains are about fifteen miles in length; in their breadth they vary from five or six to two or three miles.

Massive pieces of coarse granite, apparently in a state of rapid decay, are loosely scattered on all the more elevated spots in the plains; there are also, but lying level with the surface, frequent appearances of limestone of an excellent quality.

At about eleven o'clock, having crossed the plains, they enter the forest[19], when having travelled over a level country about five miles and a half, the face of the country, to their surprise, became at once changed, broken, irregular, and precipitous; so that it was a considerable time before they could find a route for the carts.

At three o'clock this afternoon, they found themselves on the banks of the Murrumbidgee river, having travelled from the place whence they started this morning, eleven miles S. 60 W.

The river, however, is so swollen by the late rains, that it appears utterly impassable, and it is evidently rising.

The whole of the country, on the opposite side of the river, is broken and irregular; and, from the appearance of a high perpendicular rock on the opposite bank, it is presumed that the hills on that side, are composed of limestone also. The strata, of which this rock is composed, lie some of them in an angle of 45, and some of them in an angle of about 60 degrees; but on a hill near the tent, the limestone lies

---

[18] Obliquely across the plains.

[19] This, with the southern mountains forms, most probably, the barrier of separation between the plains and Monaroo, or Brisbane Downs; discovered in the year 1823, by Captain Currie, R. N. and the late Major Ovens.

in large broken fragments, equally irregular in size and figure, intermixed with portions of a reddish earthy substance, very similar to tile.

The river is from thirty to forty yards in breadth, the water in most places level with the top of the banks. The rate of the current, at the place where they are to cross, seems between five and six knots an hour. Weather squally.

The timber consists on this side of the plain, of stringy bark, box, the manna tree, and the she-oak; the last of which is found only on the banks of the river. The greater portion of the soil is good.

Wednesday, October 20.--The weather fine except a few light showers. As the river is still rising, they are prevented from crossing it, and are in consequence detained on its banks.

Thursday, October 21.--The weather throughout fine. Waters stationary; no appearance of their falling. A party is therefore sent out to hunt, but returns without success. This river, as well as all those streams which they have already crossed, abounds with excellent fish, of the same species as that in the Lachlan, and in the other streams which run to the westward. These are in shape like the cod-fish, and of a fine flavour.[20] The thermometer at noon 70.

Friday, October 22.--No reduction, nor apparent probability of any early reduction of the waters. It is determined therefore to make the attempt without further delay, and whatever the risk, of crossing the river[21]--an operation which is literally no sooner determined upon than effected.

---

[20] These fish weigh in general from five to twenty pounds; some of them even exceed the latter weight. They take the bait readily.

[21] The details may perhaps be of some utility. The timber of the country unless dry, and there was none to be found in this state, is not even of itself buoyant, or they would hare availed themselves of it, to construct a temporary raft or boat for the conveyance of the supplies; and at this season, as the trees do not readily part with their bark, they were precluded also from having recourse to this not unusual substitute for the former. They now, therefore, but accidentally, turned their thoughts to the carts; one of which, stripped of its axle, wheels, and shafts, and securely covered with a tarpaulin, was readily converted into a tolerably good punt, or boat; this was found both sufficiently buoyant, and not too crank. The next step was to convey the end of a stout rope to the opposite bank, for the purpose of their being enabled to ply their

One of the carts is made to supply the place of a punt or boat, and the end of a tow-rope, having been conveyed across the river, in the course of four or five hours, the whole of the supplies, including the second cart is landed, without loss or injury, on the left bank of the Murrumbidgee. The horses and bullocks are now conducted separately across the stream, though not without much difficulty, and considerable risk, by means of the tow-rope. By five o'clock, every thing had been readjusted; and they rest for the night on the banks of the stream, a short distance from the place at which they had crossed. The weather during the earlier part of the day, cloudy and showery; towards evening, squalls, accompanied at intervals with heavy rain.

Saturday, October 23rd.--Immediately on leaving the banks of the Murrumbidgee, they commence crossing obliquely, and in a zig-zag course (the mean direction of which is S W.) a moderately steep but high limestone range, lying nearly N. and S. (parallel with the river at this spot) thinly wooded, but well covered with good grass. From the summit of this range, an extensive view of the river is obtained, first

---

boat backwards and forwards across the stream; and to effect this indispensable object, Mr. Hume and one of the men undertook the dangerous enterprise of swimming across the river, taking with them a small line, of about six feet long, which they carried between their teeth; and to the bite or middle of which, was attached a line of a similar description, but which was of a length sufficient to reach across the stream. This was not done without great difficulty, and some danger, both from the extreme rapidity of the current, and the great pressure of the water on a length of line so considerable as was necessary for the purpose, the weight of the latter, not only retarding the progress of the swimmers, but occasioning them to swim deeply, and at times dragging them almost under the water, and by which circumstance they were in fact, swept down the river a considerable distance, ere they could reach the opposite bank. They now conveyed one of the ends of their intended tow-rope across the river, by means of the line, and by ten o'clock, every thing being in readiness, and their boat loaded, and carrying not less than 6 or 7 cwt. made its first trip. The bollocks and horses were now conducted across separately; some of the bullocks being in a state of almost complete submersion, during the operation, and one of them becoming turned upon its back, and continuing in this position a considerable portion of the passage. These difficulties were attributable, partly to the cattle not being accustomed to swimming, and partly to the dangerous rapidity of the stream; which, with the roughness of the weather, and the unusual coldness of the water, contributed to render this undertaking to the swimmers at least, not less unpleasant than it was evidently hazardous.

forming a reach of two or three miles to the northward, when it becomes concealed by its hilly banks and bends to the westward, and then returning in a southerly direction to the western aspect of the range to a spot not more than three quarters of a mile from where they stood, forms an extensive peninsula. From this point (until it is again lost among the sloping hills and precipitous rocks which alternately form its banks) it pursues a course of about three-quarters of a mile, nearly due west.

To the south and S S E. the river is seen at intervals, for a distance of three or four miles, and beyond this an interminable extent of a broken, irregular, and mountainous country presents itself to the eye.

From the summit of the range, they continue the same course, viz. S W. descend gradually a distance of about one mile, then proceed through a hilly forest country a distance of about seven miles; at the termination of which, they meet with a second hilly range, lying in the same direction as the first, viz. N. and S. of about the same height, or perhaps somewhat higher, yet utterly unlike that range, the soil being bad, thickly wooded, and almost without grass. This range they also cross obliquely as the former, observing (to facilitate the travelling of the cattle) the same zig-zag course.

At five o'clock they have arrived at the summit of this range, on the western side of which, immediately before them, are some fine natural meadows; these they are crossing at six; walking over grass superior to any which they had ever seen in the colony.

Each of these beautiful small meadows is skirted by forest, and this again walled in by steep mountains or hills. They lie on the left bank of the Murrumbidgee, but from which stream they are separated by part of the above barrier.[22]

The trees here consisted solely of the manna tree. In the hilly ranges they had met with the box and the stringy bark; and in the limestone districts they had seen the honey-suckle, and a small species of blue gum.

---

[22] The general sward of these meadows, consists not only of a fine grass like English rye-grass, but also of other grasses, similar to clover lucerne, and burnet.

At sun-set, about mid-way across these meadows, they halt for the night, near a chain of small ponds (of good water) extending obliquely across the meadows in a N W. direction.

Their course S. 35 W. the distance travelled ten miles.

Sunday, Oct. 24.--Up to two o'clock, the day was spent in a laborious but ineffectual attempt to discover a pass through the mountain barrier in their advance. The party now separated; Mr. Hovell, with one of the men, following a chain of ponds in the direction N W. for four or five miles; when these ponds were found to form a stream, which made its escape through a chasm dividing the northern and western barrier ranges from each other. Down this chasm the stream soon precipitated itself in numerous falls, so that it became impracticable to follow it further. From one of the forest hills of the northern range, a fine view of the Murrumbidgee was again obtained at a considerable depth (perhaps a quarter of a mile) immediately skirting the range--extending in a direct course towards them from the eastward about two miles, and from them to the westward about three miles, a rapid and fine stream of somewhat larger dimensions than at the spot where they had crossed it.

They would now have returned to the tent, but lost their way in the attempt to find an emu which they had killed on their way out.

Mr. Hume, with two of the men, took the direction S W.; when, after proceeding about two miles, he met also with a chain of ponds, extending in the direction of his route; which again became a stream.-- This they succeeded in tracing, though not without much difficulty, until bending more to the westward, and descending rapidly through a deep narrow chasm it poured its waters into another stream which it met at right angles on the western side of the range. This little stream was about twenty yards wide, flowing rapidly over pebbles and loose fragments of rock. On its opposite bank was a beautiful valley, bounded on the west by a high and almost perpendicular range, extending parallel with the one through which they had just passed. Mr. Hume being satisfied of the practicability of the pass which he had just discovered, they now return to the tent, where they arrive a little before sunset. Thermometer at noon 72 deg.

Monday, Oct. 25.--Mr. Hovell had returned to the tent by seven o'clock this morning, and by five in the afternoon the whole party had descended with safety through the pass which had been discovered by

Mr. Hume, and had arrived at the precise spot where his journey had terminated yesterday. Here they remained the night. Distance travelled in a direct line, five miles and a half, about S. 22 W.

Tuesday Oct. 26.--This morning was occupied in forwarding the supplies, as well as the carts across the stream--when they again pitched their tent not far from its left bank. Mr. Hovell was now employed in making arrangements for leaving the carts, (which from the mountainous character of the country before them, it had become impracticable to take further), and in concealing along the banks of the stream such of the supplies as they perceived it would be impossible to convey on the backs of the cattle. Meantime Mr. Hume, with one of the men, proceeds in a N W. direction, in quest of a pass through the western barrier of the valley, travels five miles and then returns, at dusk, to the tent; having obtained a sight of the Murrumbidgee, along the banks of which river, they had been informed by the natives, there is a route, leading to some extensive plains in the interior. Killed a kangaroo. Thermometer, at noon, in the shade, 79 deg.

Wednesday, Oct. 27.--The bullocks having strayed, the party were not enabled to start till near noon. They now proceed about five miles and a half in the direction N W. by N.; and at half after two o'clock, arrive at the Murrumbidgee river, which having just been joined (on its left bank) by the stream they had passed yesterday, as well as by a small creek on its right bank, is here running in the direction W. by S. a broad, apparently deep, and rapid stream.

Along the banks of this river they proceed about two miles (in the direction W. by S.) when they arrive at the western border of the valley. Here they soon discovered that which, no doubt, was the route pointed out to them by the natives. But unfortunately this proved to be a mere footpath, so narrow as scarcely to admit one person at a time. Beneath which, at the depth of about ten feet, was the stream, and above it the mountain inclining not more than 15 or 20 deg from the perpendicular. This route therefore, if practicable for the men, it was too clear, was not merely unsafe, but utterly impracticable, for the cattle. They had passed some native huts about half a mile before their arrival at this spot.

Mr. Hume contrived, but with considerable difficulty, to ascend the range, whence he obtained a view of the river forming a reach of two or three miles due west; and of the country in the same direction, which appeared more level, and of a less general elevation than any which they had passed the last few days, and the hills lower, and more scantily wooded. They now retraced their steps about two miles and a half, and then halted at sunset, about five miles from the spot which they had left in the morning.

Thursday, Oct. 28.--They travel to-day 13 miles, effecting a course about due S., nearly the entire length of the valley, (its average breadth appeared to be about a mile and a half); when they found its southern extremity almost completely closed by a mountain branch given off from the western barrier range, the bluff extremity of which is washed by the same stream which they had lately crossed. The soil of this extensive valley is of a highly productive character, the basis of it being formed of the debris of limestone and of a fine granite, and this again rests upon a blue limestone, which generally, at regular intervals of between four and six feet, appears above the surface, forming long ridges in the direction N W. by N. and S E. by S. (nearly parallel with the mountains on each side), frequently extending uninterruptedly, one or two miles in length. Each of these ridges forms an inclined plane, and is about two feet in breadth, with its bluff or higher edge facing the east, and its inclined edge facing the west[23] The interstices between the ridges are thickly covered with a fine grass, which, with the bare bluff edges of the ridges present, on being viewed from the eastward, the singular appearance of small waves following each other in regular succession.

The base of the western barrier range, and about one-third of its height consist of limestone. The upper portion appears to be chiefly plum-pudding stone, resting on an interpositious layer of a species of schistous or slate. The lower part of the range appears highly productive, and on the upper division to the very summits, the grass seems good and the trees healthy, but the schistous stratum forms a broad belt, conspicuously marked by almost utter sterility.

Friday, October 29.--At sunrise Mr. Hume, with one of the men, ascends a high hill not far from the tent, in order to obtain a view of their projected route. From this is seen an opening[24] in the direction S.

---

[23] In their progress up this valley, there were observed several large and deep holes, apparently the outlets of some considerable subterranean cavities; rich, probably, in the organic remains of these regions. See Appendix.
[24] But which was discovered and examined by Mr. Hume, and therefore described on the 24th.

half W. similar, apparently, to the one through which they had passed on the 25th instant. Thither, a distance of nearly two miles, they proceed after breakfast, when this opening is discovered to be merely a mountain chasm of not more than ten feet wide. The precipitous sides of this are upwards of a hundred feet in height, and the bottom of it forms the bed of a small stream, at present about two or three feet deep. Their route up this, is of course impracticable. They now, therefore, retrace their steps about a mile and a half towards the branch of the Murrumbidgee, and then commence their ascent of the mountains contiguous to the main range, which forms the western boundary of the valley. After two or three hours of much fatigue to the cattle,[25] by pursuing a zigzag route, they arrive at the summit of the most elevated part of the range near them. This proved, unexpectedly, to be a broad flat table land, and this again so thickly wooded, that their view to the westward was utterly intercepted, while in the direction S E. which was more open, the country appeared unusually mountainous and irregular. The grass here is indifferent; the timber good. About a mile and a half from the spot at which they had reached the summit of this table-range, they encounter a fine little stream, a desirable object, the day being very hot. Here, at one o'clock, they stop to refresh, and resume their route at three, observing the direction S S W. through a country utterly dissimilar from any which they have yet noticed on their route. The soil here is not good, but the grass, if not too old, would be far from bad. The timber superior to any which they have hitherto met with; and there is abundance of excellent water. The line of that portion of the mountains on which they are still travelling, lies N E. and S W.

About six o'clock they halt for the night, near a little stream. Distance travelled eight miles.

Saturday, October 30.--The day cloudy, but temperate and agreeable. The distance travelled seven miles and a half, in a course winding from S. to W. The surface, hitherto level, is now broken by undulations, forming successive series of little hills and valleys, with here and there some flats, consisting of quagmire or bog. These are produced by the drainings from the surrounding elevations, and are the sources of numerous little streams, running to the northward and east-

---

[25] Each of the cattle had a burthen to carry of not less than three hundred weight.

ward. One of these streams, however, a fine brook, takes its course to the N W.

They yesterday passed through a small forest, full of wombat holes, and through another to-day (these spots are dangerous for travelling), and in some places the route was rendered almost impracticable, by immense quantities of dead timber. Twice had they to unload the cattle to-day--once in order to cross one of the numerous little creeks--the stream in which runs (N.) very strong; and in the second instance, in crossing one of the swampy flats, and which even then they were not able to effect without considerable difficulty. The country to the S. and S W. becomes somewhat more open than usual, and the timber always good, continues to improve as they advance. They are at present among a species of mountain gum, of the finest description. The stones found on the surface, are a coarse granite.

Sunday, October 31st.--They start at sunrise; their route, the first two miles (incessantly interrupted by swampy gutters, S. 25 W.), along the eastern border of one continued swamp;[26] the next five S W. and this also alternately broken by springs and small creeks, or wombat holes; and at other times, rendered almost impracticable by immense quantities of dead timber of the largest size, through generally, a thickly wooded and scrubby country. Between the swamp, and the latter description of country, they had met with a small patch of good grass--a timely and very acceptable relief to the cattle.

Several emus were seen on the opposite (the west) side of the swamp, but which, from its impassable nature, were inaccessible by the dogs. At one or two o'clock, they had ascended a considerable eminence; when they unexpectedly found, that they were not far from the precipitous and deep descent that forms, it seems, one of the terminations of the table range, along the summits of which they had been travelling the last three days. Their course, a distance of twenty-four miles, it was inferred, had been diagonal in respect to the summits of this range, and which they had reason to believe was, in its general breadth, not less than ten miles. From this eminence, the objects most conspicuous are, a large circular basin, at the apparent distance, of about ten miles (the bottom of which comprises some miles of level country,) and the lofty mountains which surround this spot.

---

[26] This swamp is covered with a species of moss, and has a considerable stream of water running along its centre.

22

In the direction N W. they observed smoke, supposed to proceed from the fires of the natives. This direction appears far the most favourable for their progress, but is abandoned, from the opinion that it would lead too much to the Westward, of that course, from which they are desirous as little as possible to deviate.

At two in the afternoon, they arrive at the extremity of the table range, distant three miles from the elevation just noticed. The sight of this descent was rather terrific; the idea of passing down it was yet more so. After some deliberation, however, they determine on making the attempt, not having been able to discover any other place more favourable for their purpose. About half-past two o'clock, they commence operations, by first sending down the bullocks, and in an hour and a half, the whole party arrive safe at the foot of the upper division of the descent, when, after some minutes rest, upon a rocky shelf projecting a few yards from the sides of the mountain, they recommence their passage down the second stage of the descent, which is considerably less steep than the former. At the foot of this range, in the distance, they perceive a small river, with fine pasturage on its banks, and at which, they also arrive, at about half-past five o'clock.

This stream, which is very strong, appears to run N W. and is generally, about three or four rods broad, though in some places not half so much; the banks appear to be occasionally flooded. Close to the spot where they pitched their tent was a rapid, extending in length about sixty feet, and the fall of the water in which was about ten.

The timber observed in this day's route, consists principally of the best description of the woolley, and black-butted gums, and of another species--a sort of box-gum.

From the spot at which they commence their descent, the bearings of the most remarkable mountains round them were 1*st*, a very high pyramidal mountain, S. by W. half W. distant about five or six miles; 2*ndly*, a range of mountains, terminating, not far from them at the river, apparently a continuation of that table range on which they had just been travelling; and 3*dly*, continuous ranges of mountains, extending to the utmost verge of the horizon, in the direction N W.

The total distance gained to-day, was ten miles S. 25 W.

Monday, November 1st.--Thermometer at sunrise, 50; at noon 89 in the tent. As there was here sufficient and good feed for the cattle, which had had but scanty fare, and were much fatigued by the last three days journey, they resolve to halt for the day, intending to employ themselves, in making preparations for a good journey on the morrow. A large kangaroo was killed, and a lobster was caught in the river, twelve or thirteen inches long, and of an excellent flavour.[27] They sow some clover seed, and a few peach stones, a practice which they had observed at every place at which they had stopped since the 19th of the last month.

Tuesday, November 2d.--They cross the river immediately, after breakfast, a little below their resting place; journey along the left bank, in a N. westerly direction three miles, and then, leaving the river, proceed S W. two miles along a valley, appearing to offer a passage in that direction the most desirable for them. The soil here is not very good. It was now noon, and the weather oppressively sultry, they therefore remained in this spot till three,[28] when they again advanced in the direction W S W. three miles. Considerable improvement begins to be here perceptible in the soil, the formation of the hills, and in the timber, which also stands more thinly scattered than on those parts of the country over which they had lately travelled. Kangaroos are in abundance; the grass long and fresh.

About five this afternoon they arrive in sight of some small plains to the westward, with a large stream in that direction, and an opening extending N. and S. through which, as far as it could be seen, the stream pursues its course. The timber, as they approach this river, appears to be the same as that on the Murrumbidgee, but there is no swamp oak.

A native path, bearing impressions of the feet of a considerable number of natives, including those of women and children, was here met with, extending in the same direction in which they were themselves desirous of travelling.[29]

---

[27] In size, shape, and in every respect the same as the common lobster of England, except a number of carbuncles or small nobs on the back, cuminated, as to constitute a rough or somewhat prickly surface.

[28] On the bank of a little creek, that joins the stream which they had left.

[29] These paths may, of course often be distinguished from those of the kangaroo, by the form of the foot marks; besides, those paths peculiar solely to the kangaroo, are much narrower than the former. Any of them, however, are highly valuable, being not only the best guides to grass or to water, but those

The impressions of the feet of the Aboriginal natives may be readily distinguished from those of Europeans, by the narrowness of the heel, the comparative broadness of the fore part of the foot, the shortness of the toe, and a peculiar bend of the internal edge of foot inwards (a form very probably incident to the method employed by these people in climbing trees); and the smallness of the entire impression, compared with that of a European.

Some of the trees bear the marks of iron tomahawks, obtained possibly from the stockmen at Lake George.

Having advanced two miles further, (S W.) they halt for the night. The total distance travelled this day, is eleven miles.

Wednesday, November 3.--Weather cloudy; indications of rain. They start at sunrise; proceed towards the river, and after having travelled three miles in the direction about S. 20 deg. W. arrive on its banks. This stream, which they name the "Medway," proves to be about 100 feet wide, has a strong current, and is of various depths. They proceed along the right (the E.) bank of this river three miles (S.) and then rest (at ten o'clock). Several kangaroos were seen in the course of the day. One of these was killed, weighing not less than one hundred weight. The basis of the soil appears to consist of a coarse granite; the grass good. At two in the afternoon they renew their journey along the right bank of the river; proceed two miles S. then S. 15 E. two and a half miles. The river here bending a little to the eastward, they deem it advisable to cross it; but, finding it too deep, return down the stream one mile and a quarter, where they discover a place at which the natives had apparently crossed only a few days previously.

The river, at this ford, is at least 150 feet wide, the current strong, and the water about two feet and a half deep. Below this spot, a short distance, there were some falls. They cross with the cattle, loaded, and shortly after sunset encamp on the left (W.) bank.

From the marks on its banks, and on the trees, this river is evidently subject at times to floods, when the water must occasionally rise at least ten or fifteen feet higher than its present level.

---

of the natives being frequently the only directing marks through an intricate and difficult country.

Thermometer, at sunrise, 54 deg.; at noon, 79 deg.; distance travelled, nine miles.

Thursday, November 4.--At about half past six o'clock, they again move forward, leave the banks of the river, and shape their course for an opening in the mountains, bearing S. 20 E. at the supposed distance of four miles and a quarter. On their arrival, however, at this spot (through which they had hoped to be enabled to pass), they again come in sight of the river, running in the direction N E.; and here they seem as if they were again about to be completely shut in on all sides by mountains. Two miles yet further S. they arrive at the river, where they rest about noon.

During the last four days and nights, they have been tormented by swarms of little flies; these by day, and a large species of musquito by night, were found extremely distressing.

The tea-tree grows on the sides of this river. A fish was seen in the stream, but which refused the bait. This was the first fish that had been observed in the last two rivers, and closely resembled the cod fish of the Lachlan and Murrumbidgee.

Convinced of the impossibility of pursuing their desired route, by proceeding up the river, they decide upon ascending a mountain in front of them, in the hope that it would prove to be a part of some continuous main range (that is, running N. and S.), on the summit of which (as in the late instance), they might be enabled to travel until they should discover a country somewhat more favourable for their progress than that immediately around them. After an hour and a half's fatigue, they reach in safety the summit, but which they find completely insolated from the main range, excepting at one point; and here it is connected to it only by a causeway, not more than 20 feet broad, and about 200 feet long. At this spot they encamp for the night. The thermometer 76 deg. at noon.

The natives appear to be numerous; in the course of the day, their fires were seen in different directions, and their huts or camps (which are constructed in the same manner as those in that part of the country which we inhabit) have been frequently met with; they were several times hailed, but could not, although they replied, be induced to approach.

Distance travelled, seven miles and a half, from S. 20 E. to S. 35 W.

Friday, November 5--At sunrise, having proceeded along the causeway, or ridge, they commence ascending the mountain, to which the extremity of it is attached; when having arrived about a furlong from the summit they find it necessary to unload the cattle, and for the men to carry up the loads, the ascent having become so steep, that the cattle are every moment in danger of slipping or falling, in which event they would be precipitated down this steep descent, and be inevitably dashed to pieces: the mountain, part of which rises at an angle of 50 deg. and much of it at that of 45 deg. being at least a mile in extent, in a direct line from the foot to the summit. At half past eight in the forenoon, they had completed their ascent of the mountain, which they found, as they had surmised, to consist of an extensive table land, thickly covered with timber of the largest size, (the usual species,) and of the best quality.

The cattle are now re-loaded, and they proceed in a Westerly direction one mile, when they arrive at a small stream. Here they halt to breakfast, and refresh the cattle, which had been without water during the night; none, excepting an extremely small quantity, insufficient for their own use, having been procurable.

After breakfast they again proceed, travelling along a spine, or ridge, of about a quarter of a mile broad, and which forms the central summits of this range. At six they halt for the night, having travelled, a distance of eight miles and a half; in the direction S. 45 W. to W. 10 N. The country traversed to-day, is almost the precise counterpart of the table-land over which they had just before travelled, in their route from lime-stone valley, consisting of swamps and springs, as in that instance, though neither so numerous nor so extensive. The basis of the soil which is moderately good, consists of a coarse granite. They met to-day, with pheasants, and several other species of birds, peculiar to rocks and scrubs. At a spot where they halt, near a swampy creek,[30] there is abundance of grass. The air is dry; in the day time cool; during the night cold, and there is no sign of dew.

---

[30] These creeks commence in numerous springs, which are found on each side, on the edges of the ridge along which they are travelling, boiling out of an apparently deep peaty soil, covered with a species of moss; and which having pursued their course a short distance, become strong streams.

Saturday, November 6--Weather throughout the day, cool and cloudy, in the evening showery. Thermometer, at sunrise, 44 deg. After breakfast they again renew their route, as hitherto, along the spine or ridge, which, without any observable depression or elevation, forms the summit of these mountains, winding diagonally (about S W. and by W. nearly in the direction of the course which they were desirous of making good) across the range. All the land passed to-day, in a distance of six miles, is extremely good, but the grass coarse and wiry. The timber (of the usual species) moderately thick, but of the best quality; the basis of the soil a coarse granite. They had now (it was noon,) unexpectedly reached the S W. extremity of the ridge or spine, and of this table range, which here terminates in an abrupt and very steep descent. The mountain range appears to branch off at this spot, on each side of them, viz. to the S E. and N W. but the spine or ridge along which they had been hitherto travelling, seemed here finally to terminate.

The view from this spot consists of a valley (immediately in their front S.), extending in the direction S W. and varying from one to two miles in breadth. Along the centre of this valley, runs a small stream, and immediately beyond the stream, is a broken mountainous country, and in this again, a remarkably deep chasm or opening, bearing due S. at the back of which, though apparently at a considerable distance, the view is finally closed by mountains, both of a different form (peaked), and of an infinitely greater height than any which they had yet seen.

They now descended the table range pursuing the zig-zag course of one of the little tributaries of the stream which they had observed in the valley, taking its rise in these mountains, not far below the spot at which they commence making their descent. At six o'clock in the evening, they arrive in the valley. At seven, having still pursued their course along the same branch, they come to the main stream, which having been now enlarged by the junction of a second branch, was here about four feet deep, and on the average, eight feet broad, flowing at about the rate of two miles an hour; the banks grassy, the brink covered with reeds. In effecting the descent from these mountains, they had nearly lost one of the party, as well as a bullock; the animal had fallen when it had reached about two-thirds down the mountain, in consequence of the slipping of a stone from under its feet, and in its fall, it had forced down with it, the man who was leading it. But their fall was intercepted by a large tree, and the man, as well as the animal, was thus prevented from being dashed to pieces. The man, however, unfortunately, was much hurt.

Never was the great superiority of bullocks to horses (in some respects) for journeys of this description, more observable than in the progress of this dangerous and difficult descent. The horses, it had become indispensable to unload, and to conduct with great care; but if one of the bullocks be led, the rest follow; the horse is timid and hurried in its action, in places where there is danger; the bullock is steady and cautious. If the latter slip in its ascent, or if the acclivity be too steep for ascent, in its usual mode of progression, the animal kneels down, and scrambles up in this posture. If it be descending, and it become placed in a similar predicament, it sits down, and turns its head round towards the ascent, as if to balance the body. For the crossing of unsound or boggy ground, the structure of its hoof is particularly adapted, while the foot of the horse, on the contrary, is ill suited for this purpose, and for which the fears, and consequent agitation of the animal, render it unfit.[31]

They observe several pheasants and kangaroos, of the species known by the name of the "black whallaby," a circumstance adverse to their hope of soon reaching a level country, those animals being generally the inhabitants of mountains and scrubs. Near the foot of the mountain, they notice the sassafras-tree, the fern-tree, and the musk plant, none of which are usually found so far in the interior. They halt for the night at sunset, having first crossed to the left bank of the stream. Distance travelled this day, eleven miles S. and S. 45 W.

Sunday, November 7.--The cattle being fatigued, and their backs much galled by the pack-saddles, they are allowed to rest. The day fine throughout; the grass excellent. They kill a large kangaroo.

Monday, November 8.--At half past seven o'clock they had recommenced their progress, proceeding along the stream in a S. westerly direction, the stream becoming gradually broader and deeper as they advanced. At about five miles from their place of departure, it is broken by three several perpendicular falls, each from about ten to fifteen feet in height, and between twenty and thirty feet distant from each other. Two miles beyond these falls, their progress on the banks

---

[31] Bullocks ought, when used for these journeys, to be shod; the feet, otherwise, are very liable to become disabled.

of this stream is arrested by the mountainous range forming the southern barrier of the valley, and which, on each side of it, rises precipitously out of the stream.

Messrs. Hovell and Hume having ascended, close to the stream, with some difficulty, about half the height of this range, in order to be the better enabled to decide as to their future operations, were suddenly surprised by a sight, to the utmost degree magnificent. Mountains, of a conoidal form, and of an apparently immense height, and some of them covered about one fourth of their height, with snow, were now seen extending semicircularly from the S E. to S S W. at the supposed distance of about twenty miles. The sun was bright (it was about ten or or eleven in the forenoon), and gave them an appearance the most brilliant.

The mountains which they had hitherto seen, compared with these stupendous elevations, were no more than hillocks; from which, also their form, as well as their other general characters, rendered them not the less dissimilar.

The men no sooner heard of this unexpected and interesting scene than, catching the enthusiasm, they ran to the spot where the travellers were standing, and were not less than themselves surprised and delighted at this pre-eminently grand and beautiful spectacle.[32]

The stream itself, where last seen, was running to the southward, towards the newly discovered mountains. The space between these mountains (which have been designated the South Australian Alps[33]) and the spot where they stood, consists of a mountainous and hilly region, which becoming gradually of less and less elevation, terminates midway, in a thinly wooded undulating surface, extending parallel with the mountains on either side of it.

---

[32] These are evidently part of those high "peaked" mountains, which were seen to the southward of them, just previously to their descent from the table range, on Saturday last, (the 6th instant,) and are doubtless, part of the same mountains that were seen by Major Ovens and Captain Currie, R. N. in their expedition to Monaroo, in 1823.

[33] In contra-distinction to the Australian Alps, some mountains discovered about this period, in the vicinity of Moreton Bay.

The river probably runs along this central depression, but is not visible.[34]

As they perceive, from the character of both the mountain range on which they are standing, and of the country immediately beyond them, that their progress (in the direction of these southern Alps) would be either impracticable, or attended with considerable danger, to both themselves and the cattle, they at once, instead of making the attempt, decide upon proceeding fifty or sixty miles to the westward; the object now in view, being to avoid, if possible, a repetition of those almost insurmountable difficulties by which they have hitherto been perpetually surrounded, and which appeared to be incidental solely to these mountainous regions.

They accordingly commence their new route, by re-ascending the stream, about a mile and three quarters (to the falls), and crossing to its right bank. Here they rest about two hours.

At three in the afternoon, ascending some low hills which lie across their route, they proceed west about a mile; then north, along the summits of these hills, three miles, to a little stream, a branch of that which they had left, here they remain the night. The grass good--the water equally so.

About an hour's march before their arrival at this halting place, they had passed between two small conical hills, unusually barren, (in the general acceptation of that word,) but conspicuous for the number, variety, and beauty, of the shrubs and plants--and those at that time in full flower--with which they were covered.

They had travelled this day about fifteen miles, S. 16 W. to W. 10 N.

Tuesday, November 9th.--The distance travelled, about thirteen miles. The direction of their route, S. 65 W. (the only instance of one direct course since their departure from M'Dougall's Plains,) through a fine level forest country of excellent pasturage, and well supplied with water.

The mountain ranges, the one a branch of the table range, which they had descended last Saturday, the other (a continuation of those

---

[34] It most probably takes a South westerly course, and is one of the tributaries of the "Hume," a river which it will be seen they met with afterwards.

mountains by which their progress to the southward had been just intercepted) had been in sight, almost continually, during the whole of yesterday. That on the right hand, the branch of the table range, in general perpendicular, in some places like a wall, and of undiminished height (this was much the higher range of the two,[35]) while that on their left hand, in the short distance of twelve miles, had gradually subsided almost to a level with the country over which they were travelling.

Here (at about four o'clock) the South Australian Alps were again in sight, bearing S. by E. half E.

Two kangaroos were killed to-day. One of the dogs was severely cut, and almost killed by the larger of these animals. They also met with two snakes a brown and a black one, the former of which was destroyed. Distance travelled, thirteen miles, S. 80 W.

A piece of stone, taken yesterday, from a spot near a run of water, being tested with the muriatic acid, gave indications of lime. The soil of this spot was extremely good; there were however but few trees here, and those consisted chiefly of the manna, and the honeysuckle, and were none of them, as timber, of any value.

Wednesday, November 10th.--The approach of the morning cold, the evening pleasant, but the noon sultry. (The thermometer, then ranging about 98.) This has been the state of the weather for some days.

They commenced moving about six o'clock, but had not proceeded more than half a mile, when they unexpectedly arrived at the brink of a ravine, extending in the directions N. and S. of not less than 1000 feet in depth, and the sides of it precipitous; they were compelled by this obstacle to alter their course, when having proceeded N. 60 W. a mile and a half, they again met with the ravine, but into which, with the assistance of a kangaroo path, they now were enabled to descend, the walls of it having here become broken into detached hills of comparatively moderate steepness.

---

[35] There was a view of another portion of this range, in the return route, at the distance of about thirty miles, when it was still of undiminished elevation, and equally precipitous.

The ravine, at the spot where they effected their descent, is about half a mile broad. In its course, however, it varies in breadth extending into a valley, in some places of double that breadth, while more to the Southward at the place where they had first met with this ravine, its sides had gradually converged into the form and dimensions of a mere chasm, not more perhaps than 100 yards in breadth, and the walls of which, were not merely, precipitous, but absolutely perpendicular. The soil of the valley, forming the bottom of this ravine, is in general good, possessing for its base, a mixture of limestone and granite; the grass excellent. The little streams which were found here, uniformly run to the Southward, as did all the waters which they had met with the last few days. Hitherto, they had been observed just as invariably to take a contrary course, to the Northward, and Westward. They had travelled to-day, about eight miles; the spot at which they stop to-night, is a complete scrub. The stones contain lime.

Thursday, November 11th.--[36]This morning, at six o'clock, again following a kangaroo track, they commence ascending a very high hill, a portion of the western wall of the ravine, under the impression that it was part of some main range, along the summits of which they might possibly be enabled again to pursue their route to the Southward. After having encountered every species of impediment or difficulty in their ascent, they arrive about nine o'clock on the summit, which, to their chagrin, proves to be a mere spine or ridge, so narrow and so craggy, as to be almost impassable by cattle. They therefore, no sooner reach the brow of this hill, than they find it necessary to descend on the op-posite side: this operation occupies an hour. From the craggy summit[37] of this hill, another, but more distant view of the Alps was obtained; one of the snow-capped mountains, (that seen yesterday,) bearing S E. with a mountainous or broken country, extending from the last men-tioned bearing, to W. and by N.

Having descended this hill, they halt in the bed of a small ravine, formed between this, and a similar, but smaller eminence in their ad-vance. Here they remained until three o'clock, but were utterly unable to obtain any rest, in consequence of the incessant and distressing at-

[36] The thermometer, at sunrise, 46; at noon, (in the shade,) 68; at sunset, 78.

[37] The summit consists of mere heaps of massive fragments of rock, but of what description was not ascertained. All this labour might have been spared, as they afterwards found, by passing round the northern side of the base of this hill.

tacks of the small flies before noticed; the horses retreated almost into the fires for the sake of the smoke--the dogs lay down in the water holes and the bullocks in the long grass, in order to escape from these insects. During the entire period that they have been among the mountains, the cattle have been, from this circumstance, totally unable to feed during the day, and but little at night, from the incessant and almost equally tormenting attacks of the mosquitoes. At three they ascend the small but steep hill in their front, and having proceeded about two miles (W.) across its summit (their route nearly level, through a brushy forest,) arrive at its Western side; here the land falls at once, forming a beautiful country, consisting of successive small slopes and elevations, extending from the N N W. to N. to the utmost verge of the horizon. This tract was thinly wooded, and the grass every where apparently abundant and excellent.

The waters which they now occasionally pass, take their course to the N W. Having descended this hill, they travel westerly about four miles, through a good forest country, on which the timber consists of blue-gum, and stringy-bark.

The distance travelled to-day, measured by the perambulator, was[38] nine miles and a half S. 45 W. and N. 75 W.

Friday, November 12th.--They travel to-day, thirteen miles to the southward and westward; for the first moiety of their journey, through a country utterly dissimilar from any which they have seen since their leaving M'Dougall's Plains, flat and boggy (although, from the state of the water holes, which are numerous, there has evidently been no rain a considerable time). Here, on their left, the country consisted of the terminations of the collateral branches of those mountainous or hilly regions over which they had hitherto been travelling. On their right, on the contrary, the land was only a little higher than that which formed their actual line of march; the whole thinly wooded; the timber fine, but the land not good. The second portion of their journey to-day, the commencement of which was marked, by their passing between two low grassy hills, lay through a country of an infinitely superior de-

---

[38] Here finishes the travelling on these ranges, whether of mountains or hills, which ran N. and S. The ranges met with after this period, consist of branches of the latter, bending in a Westerly direction, comparatively easy to traverse, and becoming gradually of less and less elevation, as they extend into the interior.

scription; dry, fertile, and thinly timbered, consisting of a successive series of small slopes and elevations, of excellent pasturage.

The waters past to-day, were generally standing in little pools (lying in the direction N W.), warmed by the sun; in the former part of their journey, plentiful and good; in the latter, scarce and ill tasted.

The timber was principally stringy-bark, a species of gum, and the cow-pasture box. They met with the bullrush in one of the little pools. Neither an emu nor a kangaroo have they seen since last Tuesday; they are, consequently, obliged to feed their dogs,[39] which are almost famished, on boiled flour.

Saturday, November 13.--The day throughout, oppressively sultry. They travel first W. and then S W.--in all, seventeen miles; the first thirteen miles, through a fine open forest country (here and there intersected with little creeks, or interspersed with ponds), of even a somewhat superior character to that over which they had travelled yesterday afternoon. At the end of this stage of their journey, they pass again between two low hills, grassy, and covered with trees, lying in a line with, and almost contiguous to, the southern extremity of a hilly range, extending about four miles in length, in the directions N. and S. Here they come into sight of a mount, bearing S. by W. half W. distant about four miles, which, from its very peculiar appearance, they name "Battery-mount." This is the southern extremity of a much higher range than the former, but running parallel with that range, at the distance from it of about two miles and a half. The mount is of a dark red colour, and from which circumstance, as well as its form, is an object not only very remarkable in itself, but utterly dissimilar from any other which they had met with in their journey.

Another mount is also now in sight, which was passed yesterday, and named, from this circumstance, "Friday Mount," bearing E. by N. distant from them about fifteen miles.

The whole of their immediate track, as well as all the surrounding country seen to-day, like that of yesterday, is a fine open forest coun-

---

[39] These faithful animals had been of the utmost importance to them (in procuring supplies of animal food) and continued to be so, until, in the course of the journey, some unfortunately were lost, and others disabled. Not a kangaroo or an emu is to be seen this hot weather, except in the morning and evening; during the beat of the day, they retire to the scrubs in the mountains.

try, consisting alternately of hill and dale, and similar in every respect to the Cowpastures.[40]

There does not appear to have been any rain here a considerable time, and they are obliged, in consequence, to travel two miles farther than it had been their intention, and this after sunset, for water.

Sunday, November 14.--The cattle are so much fatigued by the journey of yesterday, that they are permitted to rest. The men employ themselves in hunting, and bring home a large kangaroo, the first that has been seen for four or five days. In the course of the forenoon there was some thunder, with other indications of an approaching much-wished-for shower, but no rain. Messrs. Hovell and Hume, meantime, occupy themselves in an excursion to Battery-mount, which is at a distance of not more than two miles (W.) from their tent. This they climb to its summit, and obtain hence an extensive and fine view of the surrounding country.

To the eastward are seen those mountainous regions which they had just left (the most western borders of which, appear to be at the distance of about fifteen miles). From the S W. to the N N E. the view is bounded by a continued range of mountains, apparently consisting of two converging branches of the former, extending in the form of a crescent;[41] the greatest distance of which, to the southward, is about thirty miles, but to the northward very considerably less. Nearly west, the ranges become somewhat of reduced height; and due west, there is a break or opening, probably the outlet of a river.

All the intermediate country to the northward, southward, and eastward, has one general character--consisting of slight undulations, but interspersed here and there, more or less numerously, with conical hills, of various, but never of considerable elevation. Due west, however, there is not a hill or an elevation to be seen; but, here the land gradually dips.

---

[40] From the closeness of this resemblance, they were induced to name it "Camden Forest."

[41] Forming the section of a very considerable circle, of which the N. and S. range may be supposed to be the chord. The country within the scope of this fine view, and which is thus enclosed by mountains, is perhaps about forty miles square, and there is reason to suppose, from the general appearance, consists, entirely, of land of the finest description.

In the direction S E. the mountains, evidently a continuation of the South Australian Alps, preserve the usual character of those mountains; are peaked, and apparently, though now seen at a great distance, of their former pre-eminent and immense elevation.

Smoke, from the fires of the natives, was seen in different directions, between S W. and W. presenting the gratifying indication that the country was passable, and that they would not be unsupplied with fodder for the cattle.

But, to return to Battery-mount, the spot on which they are now standing. This is the southern extremity of a short range (not more than five or six miles in length), lying due N. and S. of moderate elevation; the upper part on its eastern aspect perpendicular, about one-third of its height; the lower portion, forming a steep slope, composed apparently of the material of the range itself, which has fallen down from time to time in the gradual progress of its decay.

The summits of the range form nearly one continuous level line, broken here and there only by an occasional chasm of various breadths; in one of which, near the southern extremity of the range, a centre portion is yet standing, *forming a wall* of about fifty or sixty feet in thickness, and of about seventy feet in height, and extending in length about half a mile, the breadth of the range.

This fragment, and the faces of the chasm in which it stands, present a favourable opportunity for observing the internal structure of the range; which was found to consist throughout, of stones of different sizes; the stones hard, heavy, of a darkish colour, in general not exceeding the size of the clenched fist; some of them, however, of four or five times that dimension; the larger stones in particular, of an elliptical form, but somewhat flattened on two of their sides, opposite to each other. These stones are held together by a hard earth, of a dull reddish colour, constituting a species of cement,[42] by which they are so firmly united, that it was with considerable difficulty any portion of the mass could be broken. This mass again appeared to be divided into regular strata, dipping about 15 deg. to the westward.

---

[42] This interstitial matter it perhaps in proportion to the stones or pebbles, which it unites, as two to one.

Some other circumstances connected with this range, and more particularly with the chasm, deserve mention; 1*st*, that the floor, or bottom of the chasm, is flat, and has the same general character as that of the summits of the range; and, 2*dly*, that it preserves the same dip as the upper strata, and which is also parallel with the line of the summits.

Monday, November 15.--The distance travelled to-day, is fifteen miles S. 25 W. Six miles from Battery-mount, they meet with a fine creek of excellent water, and a second smaller creek, or chain of ponds (as it appears at present) at the close of their day's journey; the former running S E. the latter S. The former, which they named "Battery-mount Creek," takes its rise from Battery-mount. They also pass some other pools, or chains of ponds. The whole of the country passed to-day, is but a realization of the view from Battery-mount. The soil excellent, a rich red loam, thinly wooded, and although parched, the grass luxuriant, plentiful, and of the best quality, and with water sufficient either for sheep or horned cattle.

The country extending from Battery-mount to the left bank of the creek, they named "Battery-mount Forest."[43]

The natives, it would seem from their tracks, are here numerous. Kangaroos are becoming plentiful; they succeed in killing one, as also a yellow snake.

Thermometer at sunrise, 50 deg.; at noon 80 deg.

Tuesday, November 16.--Soon after sunrise they re-commence their journey, and having proceeded three miles and a half S. (the land

---

[43] The country between the right bank of the creek and the river Hume, (a river discovered the next day,) is designated "Forbes's Forest," after the Honourable Francis Forbes, the Chief Justice of the Territory; and a very remarkable hill also, considerably the highest seen to-day, situate near the line of their route, about seven miles from the creek, they named "Judge's Mount."

Judge's Mount, it would seem, from the specimen produced, consists of a very fine sand stone, equal, if not superior, for building, to what is generally found in the vicinity of Sydney.

gradually sloping as they advanced), arrive suddenly on the banks of a fine river.[44] This was named "The Hume."

This beautiful stream is found to be not less than eighty yards in breadth, apparently of considerable depth; the current about three miles an hour; the water, for so considerable a current, clear.

The river itself is serpentine, the banks clothed with verdure to the water's edge; their general height various, but seldom either more or less than eight or nine feet, inclined, or precipitous, as they happen, by the bendings of the stream, to be more or less exposed to the action of the current. On each side of the river is a perpetual succession of lagoons, extending generally in length from one to two miles, and about a quarter of a mile in breadth. These, which are situate alternately on each side of the river, within those elbows or projections which are formed by its windings, often for miles together, preclude any approach to its banks.

Each of these lagoons was furnished with an inlet from the river, and an outlet into it; the former invariably at its higher or eastern, and the latter at its lower or western extremity.

The form of the lagoons is most frequently a crescent; the line of their course being at first divergent from, but ultimately convergent to, the stream. The spaces between the lagoons and the river--sometimes of more than a mile in breadth--are, however, irregular, as well in form as in size. These interspaces partly consist of swamps and unsound ground, which even when dry, although seemingly passable by man, are impassable, or at least unsafe, for cattle. In general these spots are thickly wooded (the trees consisting principally of the blue gum, mostly of a large growth), are overgrown with vines of various descriptions, and the fern, the peppermint, flax-plant, and currajong. The fern, the currajong, and the flax, flourish here in abundance; and the peppermint plant, (which they had not seen in any other part of the

---

[44] Mr. Hume having first discovered it, but since named by Captain Sturt, the Murray, after Sir George Murray; see appendix, No. Both Mr. Hume and Mr. Hovell, had anticipated the early appearance of a river in this direction; from the opinion that the large bodies of water which they had of late continually encountered, though all pursuing a southerly, or even an easterly course, would, from the apparently impenetrable barrier which is presented by the South Australian Alps to the eastward, ere long revert to the westward, and thus become distributed to the interior.

Colony) seems to surpass, both in odour and taste, the species that is generally produced in our gardens. From the flax plant the natives, as they afterwards discovered, make their fishing lines, and the nets which they use for carrying their travelling gear and provisions. [45]

Their method of fishing is as follows: they select the outlet from a lagoon, which generally consists of a little stream of about two feet deep, and of about five or six feet broad. Across this, at no great distance from its junction with the river, they form a palisade with small stakes, which are driven firmly into the mud, and then carefully interwoven with wattles. Beyond this palisade, at the distance of five or six feet higher up the stream, they form a similar palisade, but leave an opening midway in its length, of about two feet wide. A dam being thus prepared, the natives go into the lagoon, where it is sufficiently shallow for their purpose, and beating the water with their wattles, and disturbing it in every possible way, drive the fish before them into the dam, which on being sufficiently full, is immediately closed, the fish in consequence falling an easy prize. The natives near Western Port, use also the bark of a species of willow, which is thrown into the water, and produces on the fish the same effects as the coculus indicus. Near the river, they found the skin of a very large black snake, the original proprietor of which, could not have been less than eight feet long, the skin in its present shrivelled state being fall six feet. The bell bird is common here, and they afterwards met with the pelican.

Unable to devise any means of crossing the river, and in the hope of discovering some practicable ford, they now commence their progress (to the westward) down the stream; proceed three miles and a half, and then halt. At half past two they resume their route, but are soon compelled, from the continual succession of lagoon and swamp, to retire to some higher land, about two miles from the river. Here they travel (nearly in the same direction) about three miles, when they again, at four o'clock, encounter the river, at the foot of a conical hill;

---

[45] The river abounds with that species of cod fish which is common in all the western rivers. In the lagoons they caught a kind of bream or carp, of the weight of about two pounds, and of the finest possible flavour. The lagoons are literally crowded with wild ducks, and in the muddy bottom near the banks, is plenty of large muscles; these are inferior to those found in salt water; the natives dive for them in the same manner as they procure the mudoyster near Sydney, and these, with the fish caught in the river, seem to form the principal part of their food.

where they remain for the night. This hill is similar in form to those which have already been noticed. The internal composition, however, appears to be different, consisting (as it should seem from the specimens of it produced, and which were all derived from nearly the summit of the hill) of proportions; 1*st*, of rag-stone; 2*dly*, of quartz-mica; 3*dly*, of an extraordinary specimen of granite, consisting chiefly of quartz; these were found in different parts of the hill: the rag-stone, and the quartz-mica, a few feet from each other, and the granite in a spot somewhat lower down.

From the summit of this hill, there is a fine view of the river, which appearing and disappearing, in its perpetual windings, is visible to the westward about seven or eight miles; and excepting this addition, the view here is the same, or at least consists of nearly the same objects, changed more or less in appearance, by change in point of sight, as that from Battery-mount. At a short distance beyond the furthest spot where the river is visible, there is another conical hill, but one of the sides of which (apparently as if a portion of it had been cut away) is perpendicular and flat, like a wall. Beyond this remarkable object, not a hill is to be seen, and the country between the points S W. and N W. up to the barrier collateral ranges, is one continuous flat, studded with trees, gradually but constantly sloping in the direction of the opening between those ranges. This opening, which bore due west from Battery-mount, now bears W N W.

A large clear space in this immense forest (bearing W N W. distant about fifteen miles), they name "Fennel's Plains," after the late Lieut. Fennel. Smoke, supposed to be that of the natives' fires is seen, but at a less distance, in the same direction. Eastwardly are the bluff extremities of several collateral ranges, which proceeding from the main, or N. and S. range, in a winding course, advance various distances, into the low or flat country.

The extremities of none of these ranges appear to be nearer than seven miles, and some of them considerably more distant.

The main range is not here visible, being, most probably, concealed by the tortuous collateral branches.

Wednesday, November 17.--Messrs. Hovell and Hume take with them two of the men, and proceed seven miles further down the stream, still in search of some practicable crossing place, but without success, the stream becoming, as they advance, of somewhat increased magnitude; its banks more beautifully regular, and perhaps somewhat higher than what they had been before observed. The lagoons are nearly the same, and in consequence of which circumstance, it was possible only twice to approach the river. The soil, the trees,[46] the herbage, similar, but perhaps superior. There were no marks of floods; should the banks, however, become at any time inundated, the land, at a little distance, is sufficiently high to afford perfect security from such an occurrence.

At four o'clock the party had returned to the tent, having determined on proceeding on the morrow in the contrary direction, (up the river), in quest of the same object.

They have not taken a kangaroo since Monday last, nor have they seen an emu since their departure from "Swampy Valley." The total distance travelled to-day, is fourteen miles; viz. seven miles westerly (down the river), and the same distance on their return.

Thursday, November 18.--They travel about seven miles (eastwardly) up the river, when they fall in with their own track, at the place where they had first discovered the river on Tuesday last (the 10th). They now proceed S E. three miles; here the river takes a sweep to the E N E. There was at this time some distant thunder, and at four o'clock a violent storm of wind and rain, not far from them, accompanied with some heavy thunder-claps; this, though it passed off, induced them to stop, and they halted for the night, in consequence, at the extremity of a very beautiful flat. To-day they had travelled, by the perambulator, twelve miles; but, in a direct line, they are not more than three miles to the eastward of the spot at which they had first discovered the river.

Friday, November 19th.--They resume their route, (which they commenced the day before yesterday,) up the river (to the eastward).

The general appearance of the country, together with that of the soil, is rich and beautiful. The grass having apparently been burnt early in the season, and being now in full seed, is fresh and luxuriant, frequently as high as their heads, and seldom lower than their waists. On

---

[46] Viz. on the banks of the river, the blue-gum, and at a distance from the banks, where the soil is not so good, the box, the white-gum, and the stringy-bark, but there was no swamp-oak, the tree so universal, on the rivers to the northward and eastward.

both sides of the river, the "bell-birds" are "ringing merrily", a treat hitherto unusual, this being only the second time, that they have met with this delightful bird since their departure from the Cowpastures.

Fish and ducks are still abundant; they also meet with two black swans in the course of the day, the first they had seen on their journey.

About six miles from the place of their starting this morning, they observed a small islet of rock, lying nearly in the middle of the river; this consisted of a coarse granite, and lay in perpendicular ridges, N E. and S W. Four miles Eastwardly from this spot, at the foot of a high forest range, the stream suddenly narrows, and is in some places reduced to the breadth of little more than forty yards; this was attributed to their probable advance beyond the junction of some important branch, and which they might have passed without notice at the considerable distance from the river, at which they were frequently compelled to travel. Here, having determined on making the attempt to cross the river at this spot, they halt for the night.

The distance travelled to-day, measured by the perambulator, is ten miles, but which in a direct line, would not exceed seven.

Saturday, November 20th.--Weather fine, and extremely pleasant; this morning they cross the river: this they effect by means of a temporary boat,[47] hastily constructed (of wicker, covered with the tarpauling) for the occasion, and by four in the afternoon, every thing, including the cattle, had been landed on the opposite bank. At five, they left the banks of the stream, travelled two miles and a half before dark, and then halted on a patch of fine forest land.

The stream here, is furnished with a series of creeks, lagoons, and swamps, similar to those so lately observed and described. The back land is excellent, superior perhaps to that on the northern or right bank; the grass proportionately good.

Sunday, November 21st.--They start at the usually early hour, when having travelled one mile and a half, (four from the last stream,) among the usual series of lagoon, swamp and creek, they arrive on the banks of a sixth river. The breadth of this at the water's edge, was one

---

[47] Mr. Hovell had endeavoured to escape, in a similarly constructed vessel, some years before, from a situation of much danger, on the occasion of being wrecked on the western island, of Kent's groupe, in Bass's Straits.

hundred and ten feet, and the current as strong, as that of the former stream, but not so deep, the cattle therefore crossed with little difficulty, though it was necessary to construct a boat for the supplies. By noon, they had passed the river, when after extricating themselves from the usual series of lagoon, swamp, and creek, they resume their route, passing S. westerly, over the extremities of a range of hills, a collateral branch of the great N. and S. Alpine chain, from the Southern aspect of which, they perceive a fresh series of lagoon, swamp and creek, and at the short distance of only four or five miles from the last, arrive on the banks of another small river, similar in size and other respects to the former.[48] The banks of the last two streams, are not more than six feet in height, and there is every reason to believe, that during floods, these streams uniting with their lagoons, form immense sheets of water. The bottom of the former stream, consists of an excavation from the solid granite, the bed of the latter, was formed of rounded pebbles.

The natives, from the appearance of their fires, seem to be numerous, though none were seen. Two handsome large birds, termed by the Colonists, "Natives' Companions" were shot to-day, and some ducks. In the river, they caught some of the Lachlan codfish, and in the ponds, a kind of fish, similar to carp.

Monday, November 22.--Noon warm, morning and evening cool and pleasant. This morning they crossed the river, availing themselves of an immense tree that lay extended from bank to bank, and which with a rope stretched along it as a hand rope, formed a tolerably good bridge. The cattle are now so accustomed to the water that they pass without either reluctance or difficulty, roped together lengthwise, so that as the hindmost is entering the water, the headmost is coming out of it, at the opposite side. By half past eight they had completed the passage of the river, and had soon afterwards again started, when they advance about five miles south west between two ranges of hills. They now rest. In the afternoon they proceed ten miles and a half in the same direction, and then halt for the night. The country, traversed in the former part of this day's journey, was of the same description as that which they had passed yesterday; the grasses equally fine, and the wild flax, both in height and luxuriance, far superior. The latter portion

---

[48] All these streams are of about the same size, and their currents nearly the same. This and the latter two, we doubt join the Hume.

of the journey lay over a hilly forest land, generally not good, many of the trees bore the marks of iron tomahawks. Killed a kangaroo.

Tuesday, November 23.--The bullocks and horses having strayed, they started this morning somewhat later than usual; when, in the short distance of only three miles, having had to traverse the ends of several ranges of hills, they arrive at a fine forest. The grass good, the land excellent, and thinly wooded, with timber trees of the most valuable description, chiefly the stringy-bark and the box gum. Along this fine country they advance about three miles and a half, then stop near a spring. At three in the afternoon they resume their journey, and having travelled five miles and a half, (in all twelve miles), rest for the night near the extremity of a high range. The soil of the ranges bad; that of the level country, intermediate between them, invariably excellent.

The soil to the westward resembles much that about Battery-mount; the land low, with scarcely a hill. South westerly are seen the terminations of several collateral ranges, and to the eastward are observed numerous mountains, part of the Alps.

As they approach the mountains, as usual on those occasions, the flies and musquitoes are again becoming troublesome; to escape from which they are glad to submit to a state of half suffocation from smoke. The horses too are literally crippled from want of shoes.[49] The thermometer, at sunset, 62 deg.; at noon, 72 deg. Killed two snakes, both of a dark brown colour.

Wednesday, November 24.--At sunrise it was threatening rain; but about nine o'clock the weather cleared up and became warm, although it was then blowing strongly from the S. West. They started about six, travelled the first five miles south west, (through a forest country lying nearly parallel with the mountains) when they came to a creek. They now ascend in their way a high hill, on the northern aspect of which, as well as on that of another hill at a little distance, there was not a tree, although in every other direction, up to their very summits, both these hills were thickly wooded. This hill proved to be part of a dividing range, whence they obtain a fine view--of mountains to the eastward, supposed to be a continuation of the "South Australian Alps;" of the country through which they have just travelled to the

----

[49] On such journeys as these, there ought to be one or two mechanics--a blacksmith, with spare shoes and nails, and a harness maker.

northward; of a country to the westward, similar to that described on the 17th instant, and of an opening to the southward, through which they propose passing. The stream or creek last noticed passes out, most probably, through this opening. The entire space to the eastward, up to the very mountains, consists of an open forest country, indented along its centre by the course of the creek. The grass every where is quite withered, the land parched, and the creek nearly dry. At ten they halt on its banks;--they had travelled this morning seven miles and a quarter. At four they resume their march through a pleasant level country. The pasturage fine, some of it excellent, and in a moderately good state. Four miles and a quarter from the spot from which they had last started, they arrive at the north or right bank of another (the 8th) river. This stream, at its usual height, must be somewhat wider than either of the last mentioned; and the banks too are evidently at times flooded. The water is now low;--there are attached to it the usual series of lagoon, swamp, and creek. The banks and all the neighbouring country (which is extremely beautiful) consist of the finest possible soil; scantily wooded, but with timber trees of the most valuable description. The river comes from the eastern chain of mountains, and very probably joins the Hume, though perhaps at a considerable distance to the westward. They name this river the "Ovens," after the deceased Major Ovens, the late Governor, Sir Thomas Brisbane's Private Secretary.

Thursday, November 25.--Little difficulty was experienced in crossing the "Ovens," the water being so low, that it was found fordable in several places. The ford at which they passed was only three feet deep, and the bottom pebbly, so that although there was a considerable current, they were enabled to cross with the cattle laden. The banks of this river, are somewhat higher than those of the last two, and they appear less liable to floods.

The wild flax, (which is very similar to that of commerce,) grows here in profusion, generally about six feet high, also the native honeysuckle, and the grass-tree, both of which, (a circumstance by no means usual,) seem here to denote a good soil. At the hills near the "Murrumbidgee" as well as in the "Limestone-valley" the same circumstance was observable. Four miles and a half from the "Ovens" they reach the summits of a range, whence they obtain a view of that river, coming from East by North, and evidently deriving its waters, from part of the "Alpine Chain." One of these snowcapped mountains, is now in sight, bearing South East, distant about twenty miles, there is also a singularly formed mountain, in the same direction, but much nearer, which from its shape, they name "Mount Buffalo;" a fine level country is observable to the Westward, commencing at the distance of about five miles, and in some directions particularly to the N W. extending in unbroken tenor, to the utmost boundary of the horizon; to the southward of west, at a considerable distance, there is a range which extends in the directions, South East, and North West, at the distance of about eight or ten miles, some plains also are observed, situate most probably on the banks of the "Ovens" these they designate "Oxley's Plains" after the late Mr. Oxley, Surveyor General of the Territory. All the country in their line of route to-day, had been burned, and a little to the Westward of this line, the grass was still blazing to a considerable height. At noon having travelled seven miles, they rest near some water holes, on a small plot of good grass, which had most fortunately escaped the ravages of the flames. At four they renew their route, and soon afterwards arrive on the banks of a fine creek running to the northward, having in their way been obliged to cross the western terminations of several ranges of hills.[50] Some of these hills are covered with a kind of scrub, and some consist of large masses of rock piled fantastically, as if by art, on each other. The crossing of these ranges was dreadfully distressing to the cattle. A little before sunset they pitched their tent near some water holes. The grass good. The natives evidently numerous.

Friday, November 26.--They start this morning at half past five, and proceed S W. by S. with a range of forest hills on their right hand, (to the westward) in the direction of a hill, of which they had taken the bearings yesterday. The land immediately under this range is good, the grass excellent, the trees consist of a fine description of the gum and a species of manna tree. Having advanced about a mile and a half, they arrive on the banks of a fine creek; and about half a mile further reach another creek. These they crossed without difficulty, the latter at a convenient ford; the banks of this stream are not more than five or six feet in height, the breadth of the stream between twenty and thirty feet, and the current scarcely perceptible, excepting in those places where there are falls--it is now very low. This small stream, which they designated "Oxley's Creek," comes from the southward, and most probably, though at a considerable distance, joins the Ovens. Four miles and a quarter from Oxley's Creek, they arrive on the summits of

---

[50] In order to avoid too much westing, lest the object of their journey, their reaching Western Port (Port Phillip) should thus become frustrated.

another range of hills, whence they obtain a fine view to the northward and westward of a beautiful level open country, consisting of good and apparently even now of fresh pasturage, interspersed here and there with small plains or meadows. Hence, for a distance of seven miles, they continue crossing the western extremities of several stoney ranges, collateral branches of the mountains to the eastward, then come to another creek, proceeding most probably to pour its waters into the one which they had last encountered--here they remain till four o'clock. Two miles and a half distant from this spot (or ten from that of their departure this morning) they arrive at the top of a high hill; which, from the fine prospect that it affords, they name "Mount Belle-vue." The principal objects observed from this spot were--1st, A very extensive plain, bearing N. 10 deg. W. at the supposed distance of about twenty miles, and which they named after Mr. Alexander Berry, of Sydney, one of the most zealous advisers of the journey, "Berry's Plains." 2ndly, The two small plains, seen yesterday, bearing N. 15 deg. east. 3rdly, A fine level country, extending from N E. to 10 deg. W. and bounded between those points only by the horizon. 4thly, An unvaried succession of the most broken and mountainous regions imaginable, extending from the points south east to north east. In the direction south east, on the top of one of these mountains, there is a large sterile rock, much like that of the "Pigeon House," a well-known coast mountain to the southward. The country from south to south west, also is mountainous; but to the northward and westward (excepting a few ranges, which they expect to cross to-morrow) the country appears level. Mount Belle-vue from the foot, half way up to its summit, consists of sterile rocks, of which the strata, observing a vertical position, extend north and south.

Towards the summit, where the rock appears to contain a portion of lime, the soil and herbage are both excellent; the trees here also are large, and in addition to those before mentioned they meet with the honey suckle and the wattle. Thence they descend to the banks of another creek, where they remain the night, having travelled to-day thirteen miles and a half. Thermometer, at sunrise, 46; at noon, 88.

Saturday, November 27.--They start at six, weather at first threatening rain, but soon clearing up, and becoming oppressively sultry; proceed S W. about six miles, crossing in that short distance no less than five successive ranges near their western terminations, when the whole party, both men and cattle, being literally exhausted by fatigue and heat, they halt (at ten) near a run of water; but, on a spot where there was scarcely a blade of grass to be found. At four they resume their route and cross an extensive range, in effecting which the cattle are completely lamed. They halt, in consequence, at its foot; and where, happening to find a small supply of fodder for the cattle, they remain the night.

While crossing one of these creeks, the bank fell in, by which accident one of the horses was thrown into the water, though, excepting its lading, which consisted of provisions, without sustaining any injury.

This place appears, from the tracks that are observed, to be the resort of the kangaroo, but none are seen; and, even in the event of meeting any, the dogs are in so miserably famished a state, that they would be utterly unable to run them down. The creeks lately met with, all flow to the north west.

Sunday, November 28.--The scanty supply of grass on the spot, where they remained the night, being all consumed, they start early this morning to forage for the cattle; proceed south west, and soon arrive on the summits of a range. Here they obtain an extensive view to the N W. consisting of a level country interspersed, as usual, with plains; of a small plain or meadow to the S W. and beyond this of mountainous ranges extending completely across their proposed line of route. Having descended this range, they cross a swamp which had been mistaken for a meadow, proceed four miles and then halt on a small patch of good grass. This, like all the other spaces of any extent, lying intermediately between the ranges, consists of a kind of meadow, divided along its centre by a small but rapid stream, is somewhat swampy, and in places near the water produces reeds. The ranges, as they recede to the N. West, subside gradually, until eventually they terminate in a level country.

These meadows they named "Norton's Meadows;" and a conical mount, situate at the extremity of the range to the northward, "Norton's Mount," after Mr. James Norton, of Sydney.

The hill which they had descended in the morning was designated "Sunday Mount."

In the evening the men attempt to hunt, and meet with several kangaroos; but the dogs are utterly unable to run them down. The natives hereabouts are evidently numerous, as they conclude, from their fires, the smoke of which is observed in every direction. Yesterday their voices were distinctly heard, but none of them could be seen. Latitude, by double altitude, 38 deg. 38.

Monday, November 29.--Last night the thermometer stood at 46 deg.; to day, at noon, it had risen to 86 deg. in the shade. They start early, their course as nearly south west as the character of the country would permit. The land and timber which they observed to-day, were in general of an excellent quality, some of the soil of a pure scarlet colour and the stones nearly the same. The trees consist chiefly of the honeysuckle, the manna-tree, and the Cowpasture-box. Having travelled five miles and a half, they cross a creek running to the northward and westward, on the bank of which they rest; at four they cross another range, the whole of this range appears to have suffered by some violent explosive operation of nature. The rocks a coarse granite, lying or standing in the utmost confusion, in every possible direction; this range they descend in the direction S W. then cross another range and soon afterwards arrive at a second creek flowing also to the N W. on the bank of which they remain the night--grass abundant.

Tuesday, November 30.--They journey this morning between two ranges of hills in a south west direction, five miles and a half, then halt, start again at two (afternoon) and having proceeded two miles and a half arrive by four o'clock on the summit of a range of hills extending in the directions S E. and N W. Having descended this range, they travel southerly ten miles and a half, and then stop for the night; their progress to-day being about eighteen miles and a half.

From the foot up to the summits of these ranges the soil, the basis of which is granite, is good. The trees which they met with to-day consisted of the white gum, the stringy-bark, and the black butted gum, remarkably straight and unusually lofty. As usual, when among mountains, the small fly, so frequently noticed, has again become a great torment, and where the soil is light and loose, their route is perpetually interrupted with the burrows of the wombat.

Wednesday, December 1st.--At daylight the thermometer was standing at 41, just previously the weather had been felt uncomfortably cold; a circumstance which they had attributed partly to their present exposed and unusually elevated situation, partly to the prevalence of a south west wind. The weather which had of late been threatening rain, has now become fine. Before they descend the heights, they take advantage of an eminence, to obtain a view of the surrounding country.

Towards the east, was observed a flat forest country, apparently divided by a river; three several plains were also seen in this direction, the nearest of which seemed to be distant about four miles, the most distant about twelve, these plains appeared to be encircled with mountains in which there was a gap or chasm, the outlet most probably of some river. From S E. to south, the country is extremely rugged and broken, and it is only in the direction N W. that it appears favorable for their future progress. One mile from the spot where they commenced their descent, from the heights, they were compelled to unload the cattle in order to cross a creek, they then ascend and descend another range, when having travelled four miles and a half, in the direction S W. they arrive at another creek. Two of the dogs had left them in the course of the morning in chase of a kangaroo, and they were induced in consequence to halt at this spot, while some of the men were sent in quest of them, but who returned about sunset unsuccessful; their swiftest dog had also been absent but had returned wounded, and they had therefore but one dog remaining and this in a state of weakness and exhaustion from which it was not likely to recover.

Thursday, December 2.--This morning they are agreeably surprised by the appearance of one of the dogs that had been missing, but had returned sometime in the night slightly hurt, as they supposed by a kangaroo. At half past five (morning) they leave their resting place, and having proceeded two miles come to a meadow, divided along its centre by a creek. Hence they proceed five miles and a half S W. through a good forest country, when they are compelled to stop, the natives having fired the grass in their advance, and it being therefore doubtful whether they would be enabled to procure fodder for the cattle, if they left this spot, where there was abundance of grass and good water.

Soon after they had halted, the second dog that had been missing rejoined them, bearing on him evident marks of his having killed some animal, and by the side of which both of them, no doubt, had been lying until they had satisfactorily regaled themselves. About two o'clock they resume their route; the weather being pleasant for travelling, and the smoke and fire no longer impeding their advance.

From the summit of a hill, about a mile from the spot whence they had started, they again observe the gap in the mountains, which on Tuesday bore S E. by S. and now seems to offer to them a favourable passage; it had still, as when first observed, every appearance of being the outlet of some river. Hither therefore they directed their course, and having ascended some ranges, found the country improved as they advanced. It was however mostly burnt, and therefore not seen to much advantage; near sunset they reach a spot of about two acres in extent, on which the grass had fortunately escaped the ravages of the flames, and here they remained the night, not far from a creek. In all these creeks, where the stream was not strong, they found leeches of a large size, and apparently fit for medical purposes. They had travelled to-day, on the whole, thirteen miles.

Friday, December 3.--Proceeding S W. in the course of the creek twelve or thirteen miles, they arrive, as they had expected, on the banks of another river. The country along its sides is extremely beautiful, clothed with a luxuriant herbage, and both hill and lowland thinly wooded.

The river they cross, as on a former occasion, by means of a large tree which lay extended from bank to bank. But the access to the water for the cattle is somewhat difficult; the banks being, at least, twelve feet in height and perpendicular. The river has appended to it the usual series of creeks and lagoons, and in some places (particularly on the N. or right bank) the terminations of some high ranges come down so close to the water, that there is no practicable pass, at least for cattle. On the banks of this river they remain the night, and prepare for passing it in the morning. Some fish are caught, in the course of the evening, similar to those in the Lachlan; and they kill a kangaroo. This river has been named "the Hovell."[51]

Saturday, December 4.--By ten (forenoon) the passage of the Hovell had been completed; the cattle, as usual on these occasions, having had to cross it by swimming, and as soon as they had become extricated from the extensive swamps and creeks, which extended from its banks backwards nearly a mile, they ascend a range, the foot of which is contiguous to a creek, evidently a tributary to the Hovell. They now continue their journey in the direction S W. through an agreeable and picturesque country; the soil good, and the grass though withered,

---

[51] Originally the Goulburn, after the late Colonial Secretary. But as there was, though unknown at the time to Messrs. Hume and Hovell, another stream named after that gentleman, to prevent confusion, this river was subsequently named by Captain Sturt, and Mr. Hume as above.

abundant, studded with here and there a tree, just sufficient to afford shelter for cattle. From a hill about four miles distant from the river, they note the gap or chasm, before mentioned bearing N. by W. distant about eighteen miles; a hill which they named "Mount Throsby," after the late Mr. Throsby, Member of Council, N. 30 E. distant about five miles; Mount Meehan, named after the late Mr. James Meehan, Deputy Surveyor General of the Territory, the same distance as the last, about east; a high peak bearing S. by East, distant about sixteen miles, and a somewhat lofty range bearing S W. distant about twenty miles, and which they are desirous of reaching.

Seven miles from the Hovell they arrive on the banks of an other stream. This which is considerably smaller than the former they themselves pass with the luggage, by means of a tree and the cattle by swimming, though not without some difficulty and risque from the channel being choaked with broken trees, the depth of the water and the muddiness of the banks, from which last circumstance they named it "Muddy Creek."

One mile from the South or the left bank of this creek, they arrive on the borders of a forest, where they remain the night.

The forest land situate between the Hovell and the last stream, Mr. Hume named "Meehan's Forest." They noticed to-day some wattle-trees, that were covered with a parasitic plant the leaves of which though smaller and more closely arranged much resembled those of the peach-tree, also a species of gum-tree that was new to them, this was in full flower, and remarkably beautiful.

A finer country for sheep cannot exist than that in the vicinity of the "Hovell."

Sunday, December 5th.--Last night was the first that for some time they had found too warm, a circumstance which was attributed to the grass in every direction around them being on fire; the thermometer at daylight was however no higher than 65, though at noon, it was standing at 90, in the shade.

To-day, they halt, a matter of no small relief, to the men and cattle, they being almost alike unable to proceed.

Several fish similar to those found in the Lachlan were caught in the course of the day, and two of the men proceeded in quest of a dog that was missing, their swiftest and best, but who returned unsuccessful about dark. Latitude by double altitude, 37. 8. S.

Monday, December 6th.--For six miles together they continue crossing several ranges, and eventually ascend one of considerable height, proceed southerly, along its summits some distance, descend its western aspect with the intention of halting to breakfast, but can procure no water, and are compelled therefore to resume their journey, when after having travelled about six miles, completing twelve in all, and passing in their way several dry creeks, all of which had a westerly course, and ascending and descending a second somewhat lofty range, at two o'clock (afternoon,) they halt, having at length, fortunately discovered a small supply of that indispensable object of which they were in quest.

Their journey to-day, has been through an intricate broken country, overrun with brushwood with little or no good land excepting here and there in the hollows, this would doubtless have been avoided, had they observed only a somewhat more westerly route, a little further from the mountains, where the country appeared both clear and grassy.

The flax plant where the soil is good, is here abundant, also the lucern, and burnet, and a species of vine, the same as that which is found at Bathurst, and upon which the sheep feed in winter. The tree which is peculiar to Lake Bathurst, (somewhat similar to the native oak,) is also common here, and on the banks of the Hovell, another species of tree, which Mr. Hume recognized as the willow[52] of the colony, a very beautiful tree, especially at this season of the year. Near the tent, are some trees similar to the forest oak, which grows about Parramatta, and abundance of the Indigo Plant, to which sheep and cattle are particularly partial. To-day, for the first time since the 22nd of October, when they were at the Murrumbidgee, they experienced a fine fall of rain.

Tuesday, December 7th.--Proceed two miles and a half S W. across some ranges, and then come to a creek, which derives its waters from the mountains to the eastward; the stream strong, the bottom pebbly, and the waters evidently subject to occasional and very considerable risings. This they name the "King Parrot Creek," having

---

[52] This, which is common in Van Diemen's Land; is found only in good soil, and is there called the black wood.

54

observed here for the first time during their journey the bird of that name. They now ascend a very high stony range, lying in about the directions N W. and S E. a most toilsome task for the cattle. By nine they arrive on its summits, when they find to their great disappointment that they have to descend its S W. aspect, there being no connecting range, between this and another range, which is of yet greater height, running parallel with it, in their advance. They descend accordingly and having rested about two hours, commence climbing the next range, when after two hours toil, they arrive on the summits[53] of this also. Here, however, they find themselves completely at a stand, without clue or guide as to the direction in which they are to proceed; the brush wood so thick that it was impossible to see before them in any direction ten yards. They proceed therefore a mile and a quarter by guess, with two men ahead, cutting a route through the brush for the cattle. During this operation they were overtaken by night, and compelled to halt, utterly unable to proceed one step further: here, without water or grass, or a spot on which to rest (from the stony and rugged character of the surface,) men and cattle have to pass the night. From the summits of this range, the principal objects observed were a plain bearing N. by E. distant about four miles, and pursuing its course along the centre of this plain, the "King Parrot Creek." The plain is not very broad, of the length they were not enabled to judge. The "King Parrot Creek," no doubt joins the Hovell, about west from the spot at which they had crossed it. They were enabled to travel to-day only eight miles S W. by W. On the range they found the land-leech. This animal bites with an avidity equal to that of the water-leech. The flies and musquitoes are again extremely troublesome, and in addition the tic.

Wednesday, December 8.--After a miserable night, anxious to re-move with as little delay as possible from the causes of their discomfort, they were this morning stirring before it was day light, when proceeding one mile and a quarter in a southerly course across the range, cutting their way as they went, they at length found their further progress in this direction impracticable; both from the almost impenetrable kind of brush wood which they had to encounter, and from the immense quantity of dead timber that every where strewed the ground, as well as from the stony nature of the range itself, by which the cattle were completely crippled. They now therefore de-

---

[53] Part of a range, which they afterwards name the Jullion Range.

scend the range in an easterly direction, and in their return to King Parrot Creek, when near the bottom of the range have the good fortune to meet with a fine run of water, an object equally desirable to themselves and to the cattle, who had been eighteen hours without any. About nine they cross the King Parrot Creek; and, in the course of the afternoon, arrive at a spot where they halt, within about two miles from that at which they had crossed the same creek yesterday.

On some portions of the summits of the range, which they had just left, the soil was bad. The stones hard and of a fine grain, and here the trees were less lofty than usual in these regions; but in one spot, where the stones consisted entirely of a coarse granite, the soil on the contrary was extremely good, and the trees of an extraordinary height and girth. These too were of various kinds, and among them were some of a species of light timber lofty and straight, and therefore particularly fit for ships spars. These were found on the eastern aspect of the range. Messrs. Hovell and Hume now propose to themselves the following plan: to make a fresh attempt on foot to cross the range in a south westerly direction, and if successful to return for the cattle and persevere in pursuing that course until next Saturday se'nnight, by which time should the country yet appear unfavorable for the further prosecution of their original design, as they will then have left flour enough only for five weeks consumption, they purpose returning, and completing the outward journey by an examination, as far as circumstances may permit, of the course of the Hovell. The hoofs of the horses are sadly broken, and the feet of the cattle are so swollen, that they are at present unfit for travelling, particularly their finest bullock, the leader.

The natives here are in the habit of extracting grubs from the trees (a practice of which they had seen no trace since their leaving the Murrumbidgee). This had in one instance been done with an iron tomahawk.

Thursday, December 9th.--Agreeably to their proposed plan Messrs. Hovell and Hume start this morning at an early hour provided with provisions, except animal food, for four days. Animal food they had none not even kangaroo, for although they had seen several of these animals, they had not been able to capture any in consequence of the loss of some of their dogs, and the wretched condition of the rest.

Proceeding in a South Westerly direction about seven o'clock they were ascending a mountain, (part of the same range[54] they had ascended yesterday) which from the repulse they subsequently experienced, they afterwards named "Mount Disappointment," at ten they arrive at the top, and crossing their track of yesterday, commence descending its western aspect; two hours they were employed in scrambling literally on their hands and knees over brush and rock, when having advanced about two miles they halt, (at noon,) near a small spring; they then renew their efforts, when to add to their difficulties, they had the misfortune to encounter that species of long grass, which is known in the colony by the name of the "cutting grass," this was between four and five feet high, the blade of it an inch and a half broad, and the edges exquisitely sharp, and fine enough to inflict a severe wound. It is a similar plant to that of the same name, which is found in the Illawarra district. Uncertain of their route, fatigued, themselves lacerated and their clothes torn at every step, it had at length become literally impracticable to proceed, they now therefore return towards the tent, and remain the night near a small spring, after having succeeded in penetrating four miles into this dreadful scrub, and advanced fourteen from their station in the morning. In this scrub they found the turtine, the fern, and sassafras tree. The mountain leech was common, and the tic; which burying itself in the flesh, becomes destructive to the lower classes of animals. Pheasants they had heard, but had not seen any. The timber as they advance to the southward, is observed to be gradually of a finer appearance, but that which they met with on the mountain, a species of black butted-gum infinitely surpasses all that they had seen hitherto.

Friday, December 10th.--They start at sunrise, and at nine o'clock reach their tent, the shelter of which after their late excessive fatigues was highly acceptable. At two the whole party again proceed on their journey, and following the course of the "King Parrot Creek," pass along the plain of which they had taken the bearings the day before yesterday. This plain is a mile long, and half a mile in breadth. They travel to-day on the whole from their tent station of this morning, seven miles.

The country traversed to-day, consisted of hill and dale, both of which become more and more scantily wooded in proportion as they

---

[54] The Jullion.

recede from the mountains. The hills were observed to be stony and somewhat sterile, and the soil in general not very fine though producing a good sheep pasturage. Near their tent some rocks were observed containing a small proportion of lime; a similar kind of stone has also been met with in the bottom of the "King Parrot Creek," the latter a portion of some rocks having a vertical position, and extending in the directions E S E. and W N W. the former was found in irregular masses. Two lobsters were caught in the creek, where they seemed numerous, but no other kind of fish.

The country from "Muddy Creek," up to "Mount Disappointment," and from their tent station of this morning to the Hovell, they named after Saxe Bannister, Esquire, late Attorney General of the Colony, "Bannister's Forest."

Saturday, December 11th.--This morning they continue their progress about W N W. along the course of the creek six miles and a half, and then breakfast. At four (afternoon) they again start and leave the creek in the direction west, when having proceeded only about one mile and a half they are compelled to return, the whole of the country in this direction being on fire, and a sudden change of wind blowing both blaze and smoke full in their faces.

The country traversed consists of poor land, intermixed here and there with patches of a mountain brush, and on the immediate borders of the creek there is an irregular but generally narrow slip of good soil. The extent of which, however, increases as they advance. The country at a distance is all in flames, and the nature of its soil cannot therefore be ascertained.

Two kangaroos were killed to-day, and they caught a couple of Lachlan cod fish and destroyed a large black snake.

Sunday, December 12.--Desirous during the absence of the breeze, which they expected would return at sunrise, of passing over the scrub and grass, which were still on fire in the direction of their proposed route, they were moving this morning before five o'clock. They soon commence ascending a range and at seven o'clock, having proceeded the distance of eight miles, had arrived on its summits. Hence to the westward was observed a series of open forest hills, to the northward of which there appeared a very high forest range; here also the land in general was moderately high in the direction of the supposed course of the Hovell. To the southward the country had a similar appearance.

Descending this range they direct their march to a very remarkable forest hill, bearing W. by S. This hill, which they name after Captain Piper, late Naval Officer of the Colony, "Mount Piper," is of a conical form, its eastern aspect up to the summit clear of trees, but its other sides thickly wooded.

At nine, (forenoon) after a march of about eight miles, they came to a country of a more promising appearance, consisting of hill and dale, with a good soil well covered with grass; and wooded, though scantily, with the stringy bark and a species of gum tree. At ten they halt. At three they renew their march, and having reached the top of a hill, obtain a view of a finer and more accessible country in their advance. The country on fire in every direction. At five, having proceeded about the distance of twelve miles and a half, they stop near the banks of a creek. This they name "Sunday Creek." The mosquitoes and flies are still very troublesome. They had the misfortune, to-day, to lose a second dog. The animal had been cut in the conflict with the kangaroo that was last killed, and had very probably remained behind to rest, in consequence, until it was too late to follow.

Monday, December 13.--They travel to-day sixteen miles; the first seven miles upwards along the creek, (when meeting with a practicable ford they cross it.) The remainder of the distance in the direction S. by E. The land on the banks of the creek was not good, the grass was scanty, and the timber indifferent. In the latter division of their journey they had to traverse several ranges, the last of which, the Jullian, so named after a friend of Mr. Hovell's, appeared to be what is termed a dividing range; the waters of which, on the north side, run to the northward, (most probably to join the Hovell). Those on the southern side proceed to the southward, and very probably discharge themselves into the sea. The weather this evening was extremely cold, the wind from the S W., the thermometer 50 deg. The willow of the colony is frequently met with here, and has a beautiful appearance. At a distance it looks not much unlike the orange or the lemon tree. The indigenous flax plant also is abundant, and the bronze-winged pigeon and the king parrot are both of them common, as also the native dog.

Tuesday, December 14.--Travel twenty miles in a southerly direction--the first part of their journey through a meadow of some miles in circumference, thence up a high insulated hill, named Bland's Mount, from which they obtain a view of several extensive plains, reaching from W to S E. separated from each other by patches of forest land. To the southward the country appeared level, but interspersed here and there with hills of a conical form. The soil in all this tract of country was excellent. These plains, as well as the mount, were named after their friend, Mr. Bland of Sydney, "Bland's Plains." Thence they proceed eight miles S S W. in quest of water, but without success; until on sinking a well, about three feet deep, and forcing a pole into the earth about three feet deeper, they had the good fortune to procure water enough to afford to each of the party about half a pint, a most acceptable supply, although it was so scanty, as well as indifferent and muddy. Wherever the land in these plains rises a little above the general level, it is stoney, and in these spots it was thinly scattered over with the honey-suckle of the colony. At the end of this stage of their day's march they ascend another hill. Here the perambulator was broken to pieces, and from this circumstance the hill was named by them "Mount Odometer." From this hill, between the points S E. and W., alternate plains and forests are seen extending to the utmost verge of the horizon, and from N N E. to S E. part of the Alpine Chain; while towards the south, the land gradually dips.

Nothing could surpass the beauty of this view. The trees which they met with to-day, were nearly the same as those observed in their journey yesterday. The whole country, however, had evidently suffered from drought. The earth, even in places the most likely to be supplied with moisture and to retain it, was parched and cracked, and presented frequent chasms, wide and deep, and consequently dangerous for travelling.

At six they halted on the banks of a creek[55] which runs to the southward. They had to regret to-day the loss of another dog, a little terrier. This animal had been very useful in discovering game, and was a general favorite. It had very probably been killed by the native dogs, which are here numerous. To-day a snake was killed of a light brown colour, different therefore from any they had yet seen. They also met with the blue mountain parrot, the first they had seen since their leaving home.

The thermometer, in the morning, 60 deg.

Wednesday, December 15.--The cattle were so much fatigued by the journey of yesterday, that they were not enabled to travel till nearly

---

[55] Relief Creek.

nine o'clock. They now proceed S S W. four miles, when they come to a deep creek. This they name "Broughton's Creek," after the late Mr. Broughton, deceased, formerly Assistant Commissary General of the Colony. The course of this creek is about S., the waters apparently motionless, the banks fifty or sixty feet high, and in some places perpendicular; its waters apparently derived from part of the Jullian range to the north west. At the distance of six miles from the first creek, or two miles from the last in the direction S W., they met with a third creek. Here there had evidently been some natives not long before them. They now travel about twenty miles along a continued plain, (on which there was scarcely a tree) when they arrive on the banks of another creek or river, considerably larger than even the first which they had crossed to-day, and the banks of which were high and steep like those of Broughton's Creek. On the edges of this river they found a plant, called in the colony the sea-marigold.[56] Eels also were caught in the river, a fish which they had never found in any of the waters which flow to the westward. The soil is excellent, and the general aspect of the country highly promising. Water plentiful. The only want observable is that of timber for building; for fuel there is abundance. The sun has been obscured the last three days. It is now blowing strongly from the westward. The weather cold and dry. The thermometer ranging from 50 to 62 deg.

Thursday, December 16.--This morning they crossed the river or creek without difficulty, the water not taking the cattle more than chest high. Mr. Hume named this stream the Arndell, after the late Dr. Arndell, the father of Mrs. Hovell. They now proceed S W. by S. through the plains about six miles, when they were struck with an appearance, respecting which they could not decide, whether it was that of burning grass, or that of distant water. They now proceeded S. and at four o'clock, had the gratification satisfactorily to determine that the appearance which had just now created so much doubt, was that of water; and which, leaving the river a short distance, and directing their march from S W. to S S W. they soon ascertain to be part of the sea,-- the so long and ardently desired object of their labours. They now again alter their course to S W., and travel six miles in that direction along the shore, over excellent land, but quite clear of timber.

---

[56] A species of Mesembryanthemum.

61

On the downs or plains to-day, they had seen several flocks of emues, and wild turkeys. The kangaroo however was seldom met with. Indeed this animal is not generally found in so open a tract of country, as that over which they have been passing the last three days.

The water near the shore was covered with water-fowl, of various descriptions, some of which were new to them.--And by the time they had halted for the night, they had procured an ample supply of black swans and ducks. They stopped for the night at seven o'clock, in a small wood about a mile from the beach, but where there was no fresh water; having travelled to-day, upwards of twenty miles.

Friday, December 17th.--Indications of rain, terminating in light showers. Wind high from the westward. They proceed this morning from the beach, in a direction about N N W. three or four miles, in quest of water, when they arrive on the banks of a creek,[57] where they had the good fortune to find abundance, both of good water and of grass. Here therefore they remain the day, in order to refresh the cattle, who were not a little in want of this timely relief, more particularly as it is proposed to commence their return to-morrow. This determination of so soon retracing their steps, though it cost them much regret, had become indispensable, not only from the extreme[58] scantiness of their remaining supplies, and the certainty of the many difficulties they would have to encounter, but still more so from the consideration that the mere circumstance of a fall of rain, by swelling the streams, might in the weak, and ill-provided state, to which the whole party were re-duced, render their return altogether impracticable. This morning, one of the men, James Fitzpatrick, having proceeded a short distance up the creek, to shoot wild fowl, was suddenly surprised by a couple of natives who were lurking behind some reeds; the man no sooner per-ceived them, than he begun to retreat, and they to advance, throwing off their cloaks, and with their arms in their hands; perceiving this, he turned and snapped his piece at one of them; but as it missed fire, he had no resource left, except flight, and which also would have been unavailing, had not his shouts for assistance, brought him timely aid.

---

[57] Or at present a chain of ponds, commencing at Mount Wollstonecraft, and terminating after a course of seven or eight miles in the sea. This they named Kennedy's Creek.

[58] Four week's flour, at reduced allowance, and a small quantity of tea and sugar, but no animal food; independently of which, the ropes and other mate-rial employed for crossing streams, were now almost utterly unfit for use.

About two hours after this occurrence, as two of the people were employed in procuring fire-wood, in a small clump of trees, not far from the tent, two natives sprung towards them from behind the trees. These, however, on the men presenting their muskets at them, made signs of peace. Mr. Hume who was at hand now approached, when laying down his arms, and beckoning to the men to do the same, the natives followed the example, and after much conversation, but of which not a word was understood by either party, they proceeded with Mr. Hume to the tent. These people by degrees began to be a little better understood, when they seemed to wish to describe[59] that a vessel had been in that bay, and that the people had landed; and to imply that both the master and the people were continually in a hurry.[60] They also appeared to point out where the vessel lay, and suiting "the action to the word," endeavoured to explain that they had seen men felling trees in that direction, and this was all done with a gesture and grimace, evincing that these people were at least not bad mimics.

These natives, who were soon joined by a third, it was discovered were inquisitive, troublesome, and great thieves, cunning and treacherous. They made a laugh of the circumstance of one of the people having been pursued, though there could be no doubt as to the hostility of their intentions on that occasion. Messrs. Hovell and Hume, had been desirous of taking their horses in the direction of what they supposed to be Port Phillip, but the conduct of these people, and the numerous fires which were being made around them, apparently as signals among the natives, made them conclude, that it would be unsafe for the party to separate.

The natives here, in their form and features, very much resemble those about Sydney, their manners and customs appeared very similar, and they have the same kind of weapons. Their language however

---

[59] Alluding however very probably, to the original settlement, of Port Phillip, and when it appears in the account given of that event, that the natives were so troublesome, it became necessary to fire on them--a circumstance, which must have taken place, not far from the very spot, where the present party of discovery, was now encamped.

[60] A notion perhaps formed from the mere routine labour, or employment of the settlers, and which, compared with their own habits of indolence, and their utter ignorance of labour, might wear that appearance.

seemed totally different, as to words, from that of the Sydney natives, or those about Jarvis's Bay, though in sound,[61] it is much the same.

They did not seem astonished at the horses or bullocks, though evidently much afraid of the latter, and even dreadfully alarmed, if the bullocks, although at a considerable distance, were looking towards them.

The harbour or bay consisted of an immense sheet of water, its greatest length extending E. and W. with land which seemed to them an island, to the southward, lying across its mouth, but which, in fact, is a peninsula, with a very low isthmus connecting it to the western shore. Hence the mistaking of this spot, Port Phillip, for Western Port, a bay about fifteen miles to the eastward of the latter.[62] This error has been since satisfactorily rectified by Mr. Hovell, in his examination of Western Port, and its vicinities, on the occasion of the late settlement of that place; a short account of which will be given in the appendix.

The soil throughout the plains appeared good, in some places of considerable extent, and to afford a particularly fine dry sheep pastur-

---

[61] E.G.-

The name of the bay	. . . Geelong.
--Mount Wollstonecraft	. . . Woolloomanata.
--The downs extending to the beach	. . . Iranmoo.
Water	. . . Goolamoo.
A certain bird	. . . Bonering.
A dog	. . . Narranuke.

[62] Which in no way effects the important results of the journey, and was scarcely at the time, and with the circumstances under which it was made, to be detected or avoided, there being then no account of the localities of Western Port, at least, that could be depended on; the outline of it by Flinders, being incomplete, and the chart of Baudin, from the surreptitious manner in which it was got up, until confirmed by more respectable testimony, scarcely worthy of attention; while they themselves, were unprovided with instruments, in a fit state, as mentioned in the preface, to enable them to correct the longitudinal inaccuracy.

age. There is however a deficiency of trees fit for building,[63] though abundance for fuel. Ridges of stones, here and there intersect the plains, varying in elevation from two or three to five or six feet, and of perhaps fifty or sixty feet in breadth.

The stones are of various sizes, broken, angular, extremely hard, heavy, and some so large that they would weigh upwards of four or five hundred weight. Two such ridges as above described, extend from Mount Wollstonecraft[64] a distance of six or seven miles, almost in a direct line, nearly down to the beach. Mr. Hovell took from the root of a tree, which had been recently blown down, a piece of very soft stone, consisting almost entirely of lime; and the banks of the creek, near its entrance into the bay, seemed to consist principally of beds of shells; emus are numerous every where on the Downs, and near the sea the Cape Barren goose. The bay too is literally covered with black swans, and various other aquatic birds. Caught some black bream in the creek. Messrs. Hovell and Hume each marked his initials on a tree with an iron tomahawk, at some distance from the left bank of the creek, about two miles from the beach.

Wind high from the N W. and S W. since Sunday. Thermometer from 55 to 60 deg. at noon; in the morning 45 and 50 deg.

Saturday, December 18.--This morning they commence their return,[65] keeping between two and three miles to the southward and eastward of their outward route; at four, having travelled about fifteen

---

[63] On the Alpine Chain and the Jullian Range, there is abundance of timber fit for that purpose.

[64] The position of this mount will be given in the Journal of to-morrow.

[65] But previously to so doing, took down the following bearings, from the extremity of a low neck of land, extending a considerable distance into the bay, on the left side of the entrance into the creek, viz. The supposed entrance to the bay, but in fact a low Isthmus, S. by E. distant about fifteen miles. A bold bluff bank, part of the peninsula, forming the southern border of Port Phillip, but now mistaken for an island, distant about ten or twelve miles, S E.--High land, distant between 20 and 30 miles S. 45 W.--Mount M'Intosh named after our late Barrack-master, N. 76 E.--and Mount Campbell, after the late Mr. W. Campbell, of Harrington Park, N. 85 E. distant between 30 and 40 miles, Mount Wollstonecraft, named after Mr. E. Wollstonecraft, of Sydney, N. 25 W. seven miles, Mount Berry, named from Mr. Alexander Berry, N W. fifteen miles, and finally the Jullian Range, extending in the form of a crescent, from N E. to N W. distant at its nearest point, about seventeen miles,

miles, they halt on the banks of a large creek, taking its rise in Mount Wollstonecraft, and which they named "Dickson's Creek," after Mr. John Dickson,[66] sen. of Sydney.

Sunday, December 19.--They re-cross the Aradell, a short distance below the spot at which they had first met with it; on the following day they renew their course along the downs in the direction N E., cross Broughton's Creek,[67] and stop for the night at that chain of ponds, which they passed on the 14th instant in their outward journey; next day cross Bland's Plains, and in evening regain their former quarters in Tempe Valley.

Wednesday, December 22.--They re-cross the Jullian Range by the same pass[68] by which they had entered the downs on the 13th, and taking a northerly direction, travel successively through an extensive scrub, some fine forest land and a beautiful plain[69] a few miles to the west of their outward route, on the 12th, and halt for the night on the left bank of Sunday Creek. The following day having crossed Sunday Creek and a small stony range stretching obliquely across the line of their route, proceeding still northward, through a track of fine country, they arrive on the left bank of the Hovell, about twenty miles lower down (or more to the west) than the spot at which they had before crossed that stream, on the 4th of the present month. The river here was about seventy yards broad, apparently deep, and without any perceptible current, (but its waters had, it was evident, been greatly reduced by the late drought). Tracing it upwards about a couple of

---

[66] To whom the colonists are indebted for the first introduction of the steam-engine into the colony, in the year 1814.

[67] The banks of this creek are, in general, steep and lofty, in some places from 50 to 100 feet high, so that they could find only one spot where they could cross it. The soil throughout the downs is invariably excellent. On the 30th they met with several large fragments of granite lying loose on the surface near the creek, where they remained for the night.

[68] Hume's pass. This lies between two remarkable hills, Mount Disappointment, to the eastward, and another named Mount Wentworth, after the late Mr Wentworth, of Sydney, to the westward, about equa-distant (10 or 12 miles) from each. The whole of their route, from Port Phillip thus far, has been over fine land, consisting of Plains and Downs, fit for every purpose of grazing, and agriculture.

[69] Ornamented with clumps of that beautiful tree, the native Willow and from which circumstance, they were induced to name it Piper's Park.

miles they were so fortunate as to find a convenient ford, where the water was only about three feet deep, with a current not exceeding a mile an hour.

The whole line of country to the west of their route from Hume's Pass as far as the Hovell consists of a high broken surface, and beyond this were observed continuous ranges of considerable elevation, extending in the directions N W. and S E.

Friday and Saturday, December 24 and 25,--were spent on the banks of the Hovell, in order that they might avail themselves of the fine fish which abound in its waters, as well as refresh the cattle. In the evening of the 25th Mr. Hume's mare was bitten on the nose by a snake, and became immediately a shocking spectacle, the head swelling so much that the eyes were quite closed. An attempt to bleed having failed, half a pint of spirits of turpentine with some water was given, and about twenty minutes after, at which time the swelling had began to subside, some *eau de luce* properly diluted was also administered. Half an hour from this period the swelling had become considerably reduced, but covered with small bladders containing a thin sanious fluid; sight was restored and the animal was in every respect rapidly recovering;--as, however there still remained some sickness or nausea, with a thick viscid phlegm flowing copiously from the mouth and nostrils and much drowsiness, in order to prevent the animal from sleeping, she was kept walking gently during the whole night.

They obtained from a hill a fine view of the river flowing from the N E. through a gap in a mountain range, distant about 8 or 10 miles, when after making a considerable curve to the west,[70] it eventually turned to the N W. in which direction it was visible to a great distance. To the south the land was high and broken, to the west moderately so; from that point towards the north, the country was low but undulating.

---

[70] This is no doubt the most southern bend of the river, and is the spot where they very unexpectedly met with it on the 23rd. The Hovell, thence, from what has been said, as well as from what was to-day again observed of the country to the westward, it is only reasonable to conclude, must take a N W. course; and is therefore identical with the most southerly of those streams, seen in his late journey, by Captain Sturt, flowing eventually into the lake Alexandrina.

From N E. to S E. was seen a lofty range, forming for a considerable extent the left bank of the stream.

Sunday, December 26th.--The mare being sufficiently recovered, they resume their journey, and proceed N. half W. ten or twelve miles, for the most part through a fine undulating forest country, similar in some places, to the Cow-pastures; and abounding in kangaroos, but of which circumstance they could not avail themselves, from the disabled state of their only remaining dog. The timber met with to-day, was in general good. The views[71] of the country to the N W. and N. resembled those of yesterday. Halt for the day at two o'clock in the afternoon, (the mare being unable to proceed further) near a chain of ponds, in a fine meadow, as they conjectured, about 25 miles W. of their outward track.

Monday, December 27th.--Route about twenty miles, N E. half E. the country in general level, but not fine, studded here and there with the Cow-pasture-box, stringy-bark, and the blue-gum, but which were neither numerous nor large. Towards the west, a fine country like that of yesterday.

Tuesday, December 28th.--Thermometer, at noon, in the shade, 86. Route N E. about fifteen miles over good land, scantily wooded, and intersected here and there, by ponds and small streams. The horizon from W. to N E. a perfect level, with but one hill observable in all that distance. Ranges still terminating abruptly on their right (towards the S E.)

Wednesday, December 29.--Their course to-day was about N E., 15 or 16 miles over a level forest, with here and there a small creek, flowing towards the N W. The soil excellent, and the trees numerous-- a stunted species of blue gum. They recrossed part of Norton's Meadow, and the strong stream, thickly bordered with reeds, which runs through it.

Thursday, December 30.--Weather warm, they travel about 20 miles N E., traverse a very high barren collateral range, extending nearly due N. and by W., from which they obtain a distinct view of that remarkable mountain, named, *from its peculiar configura-*

---

[71] A plain on the banks of the Hovell, distant to the N W. about ten miles, Mr. Hume named after Mrs. Hovell, Esther's Plains.

tion, Mount Buffalo, bearing E.; and then passing through a fine scantily wooded country, they cross and stop on the right bank of Oxley's creek. The whole of the country near this creek is of the finest possible description, fit for any purposes, whether of grazing, or of agriculture, and they had reason to believe, that it was of almost unlimited extent.

Friday, December 31.--Weather cloudy, with thunder. This morning they rejoin their former track, and proceed along it in a direct course for the Ovens, at a spot where they had before, in their outward journey, forded that stream.

From a high barren collateral range, stretching N W. between Oxley's creek and the Ovens, they again had a view of Mount Buffalo, and of a continuation of the Alpine Chain towards the N E. Just before sunset they cross the Ovens and then immediately halt for the night; having travelled about fifteen miles. They caught abundance of fish in the river, and killed this day a species of adder, of a dingy brown colour, remarkable for the amazing breadth of its head.

Saturday, January 1.--Weather hazy, several light showers in the night, and distant thunder indications creating no small anxiety, and which had they been realized, would have rendered it indispensable, most probably, to have recourse to the mountains, in order that they might be enabled to head those numerous streams which they would otherwise have yet to encounter; and the passage of which during floods to them in their present state of weakness, and deprived as they now were of all the material indispensable for that purpose, would doubtless have been utterly impracticable; while a circuitous route among mountainous regions, was to them nearly destitute of provisions,[72] almost equally an object of apprehension.

They now therefore hurried along N E. for the Hume, in their old track, making a forced march of about 20 miles.

Sunday, January 2nd.--Weather cloudy; the horses having strayed in the night, they were not enabled to move this morning until six o'clock, when journeying about eight miles, they met with a considerable number of native women and children, perhaps about thirty. The children were engaged in play, throwing small spears, formed of reeds,

---

[72] Except a couple of kangaroos, and a few chance fish, animal food of any description, they had not tasted since the 25th of last month.

at a circular piece of bark, about a foot in diameter, while it was roll-ing along the ground; and the women were employed in spinning the native flax, one of whom, (an old woman,) gave immediate notice of their approach, crying out white man! white man! minija! minija! which in the language of the natives of the Murrumbidgee, would im-ply "make haste, make haste," when the whole party rose, and in a few minutes disappeared. About sunset, they crossed that branch of the Hume, which they had first passed, on the 22nd of November.

Monday, January 3rd.--Arrived at noon, after a march of about eight miles, on the right bank of the Hume, having previously crossed that branch of this river, which they first met with on the 21st of No-vember. The Hume, as well as this tributary stream, was now so low, in consequence of the long continued drought, that they were both eas-ily fordable, their waters not exceeding at their respective fords, three or four feet in depth. Shot some black swans, and ducks, and caught abundance of fish. They were induced to let the cattle rest, in conse-quence of their having reached the Hume, the principal object of their anxiety, and found it so favourable for their passage, the fineness of the weather, and the enfeebled state of the cattle.

Tuesday, January 4th.--In consideration of the extreme heat of the weather, and the weak state of the cattle, they did not leave this fa-vourable spot, until the afternoon. They now cross the river, about a mile higher up, (more to the east,) than their former crossing place, travel about two miles, still upwards, along its banks, and then halt for the purposes of fishing, shooting, and refreshing the cattle. Some of the fish, which were similar to those in the Macquarie and Lachlan, described by Mr. Oxley, were not less than thirty or forty pounds weight.

Wednesday, January 5.--They proceed about twenty miles; three or four miles up the Hume, to its junction with Battery Mount Creek, whence by their observations, they were enabled to come to the con-clusion, that the Hume receives the waters of that stream, from which they took their departure on the 8th of last November, and which pur-sues its course along the central line of that thinly wooded undulating surface at the base of the South Australian Chain, described in that day's journal. The Hume now bending to the S E. they were induced to leave it, proceeding about N E. through a good open country. During this day, they passed Battery Mount, bearing W. distant eight or ten miles.

In the afternoon they surprised a large body of natives, but who fled with precipitation. They rested for the night, in a hilly country, a few miles to the west of Friday Mount.

Thursday, January 6th.--Thermometer at noon in the shade, 76. They travelled about 16 miles, N E. through a fine open forest[73] country, scantily studded with the manna and the box. The wood of the latter is highly serviceable for the construction of fences, the spokes of wheels, and for building. The stones here consisted of Granite and Schistus; the grass was abundant and good, although the country had evidently been parched by a long continued drought.

In the course of the day, they again came by surprise upon a body of natives, consisting of eight men; these appeared much alarmed, and, on perceiving the bullocks, fled through a small creek, and concealed themselves among the reeds on its banks. In the evening, about a mile from the spot where they had been first seen, the natives again made their appearance, and approached them with marks of friendship. One of these men dressed in an old yellow jacket, spoke a few words of English, and had been at Lake George. They had among them, one iron axe, and four tomahawks.--The whole party remained with them till dark, when, except two of their number, they all retired, promising to return in the morning.

Friday, January 7.--The thermometer at daylight 46 deg. a dense fog. The natives now returned with a considerable augmentation to their numbers, amounting altogether to not less than forty able bodied men, all armed. The horses having strayed, two of the people assisted by two of the natives were employed a considerable part of the morning in bringing them in. The natives, when they were just going to start begged the travellers would accompany them to their camp, about a mile further up the creek, so that the women and children might have an opportunity of seeing them. Mr. Hume, taking three of the men with him, complied with their request, when he met with a party of about thirty women, as many children, and some fine young men. These were extremely pressing, that he and his party should remain with them, as they were going they said, to have a "Corrobera," two of them promising, in event of his compliance, to accompany him and his party, the following day as far as the Murrumbidgee. The men were the finest natives, they had ever seen, one of them about six feet high,

---

[73] Camden Forest.

and another whom they measured, five feet, nine inches and a half.--
They were all robust and well proportioned, and possessed what is unusual among the native tribes, well formed legs--Some of them had
higher foreheads than are generally observed among these people.
Their weapons are like those of the natives of the Colony, except the
spears, which were made of strong knotted reeds, about six feet long,
to which was affixed a piece of hard wood, about two feet in length,
with a rounded point, barbed in some instances, with numerous small
pieces of flint or agate. Each of these people was furnished with a
good ample cloak of opossum skin, many of them had necklaces, made
of small pieces of a yellow reed strung with the fibre of the currajong,
the flax-plant, or the hair of the opossum.--At nine they took leave of
their Camden friends, who appeared to be a kind and inoffensive people. They travelled to-day about fourteen miles, N E. the former half of
their journey still through a fine country, the latter over a tract of country traversed by several lofty, barren, slaty, collateral ranges, running
nearly N. and S.[74]--branches of the table land, passed on the 5th and
the 6th of November. In each of the valleys between these ranges there
was a small stream, or chain of ponds. The timber observed to-day was
principally the stringy-bark.

Saturday, January 8.--To-day was served out the last of their provisions, viz. six pounds of flour to each man, and some tea, while they
had a journey before them of at least a hundred and fifty miles to the
nearest stock station, over a mountainous and difficult country, and
with cattle so fatigued and crippled, that they were able to make only
short stages. They travel to-day about fourteen miles N E., still passing
over the terminations of lofty collateral schistous ranges of the same
character as those of yesterday. On one of these ranges, for the first
time since their leaving the country about Bargo River, they met with
the iron-bark tree. They had never once met with the apple-tree.

High ranges to the N W.

Sunday, January 9.--They continue journeying N E., winding
along the hollows, and over a repetition of collateral stony but grassy
ridges, extending in the usual direction N W. As usual, they met with

---

[74] Dividing ranges extending between the waters of the Murrumbidgee, and
the Hume, which streams it should appear from Captain Sturt's report, eventually unite their waters in a low level country, about a hundred miles to the
westward.

water in the hollows. Natives' fires were seen several times to the N W., where the country appeared to be an open hilly forest. In the evening they again had a sight of Ben Lomond, bearing about S E., and at the distance perhaps of twenty-five or thirty miles. They had seen this remarkable mountain a few days ago, bearing about E N E.; from one of the ranges to the N E. of Camden Forest, and when it was supposed to have been not less than seventy miles distant. The men were now so distressed from want of shoes as to be hardly able to travel. The distance travelled is not specified.

Monday, January 10.--Their course averaged to-day about a N E. direction, and they halted in the evening on the left bank of the Medway, about twenty miles N. of the spot at which they had crossed on the 3rd of November, and just below the conflux, on its right bank, of a fine little stream, which they had crossed on the 2nd of that month. The Medway here is a beautiful river winding N. through rich alluvial scantily wooded plains, known by the native name Doomot.[75] This stream, in its present very reduced state at the place at which it was forded, was three feet deep, and its current about two miles an hour; the bottom consisted of pebbles.

In the course of the day they crossed several rather high collateral ranges of coarse granite, the surfaces of which were in a state of advanced disintegration, and over a country consisting generally of poor land.

They would now from their repeated observations of the form of the country, gladly have followed the Medway to its junction with the Murrumbidgee (a circumstance of which they had no doubt, both from the observed direction of these streams, as well as from the character of the country through which they pursued their course) and then have made the easting part of their route, up the right bank of the latter river; but were deterred from this attempt, as well from their uncertainty as to the distance they would thus have to travel, as from their anxiety to rejoin the carts for the sake of the supplies which they had left with them.[76] Caught some fish of the usual description.

---

[75] The natives pronounce this word Toomot, or Doomot.

[76] It would indeed have been well, had they pursued a N N E. course, all the way from Camden Forest, until they met the Murrumbidgee, which would then have been at its junction with the Medway--as they would then have

73

Tuesday, January 11.--Crossed the river at nine o'clock, some fine open country, then two high collateral forest ranges, when they came to some rich meadow land. This being the last spot favorable for refreshing the cattle, that they had reason to expect they should meet with on this side of the mountains, they were induced to halt here after making a short stage of not more than five miles, about east, towards the western side of that table-land which they were occupied in traversing from the 29th to the 31st of last October, inclusive. Kangaroos were seen in abundance during the last two days; but of which circumstance they were not enabled to avail themselves, having now only one dog left, and this animal in too low a condition for hunting.

Wednesday, January 12.--Weather still fine but warm. Finding no practicable spot for ascending the table-land, they now pursue a S E. course in the hope of discovering one in the direction of that little tributary of the Medway, which has been just mentioned;--meet with this stream, pursue it upwards of two miles, and then commence ascending the mountains in an easterly direction, winding in a zig zag course along part of a large collateral ridge until after two hours arduous toil, and with much danger to the cattle of falling into the numerous ravines which presented themselves in their way, they had managed to climb about two thirds of the ascent. Here they halt on a tolerably flat surface, where they meet both with good grass and with water. In one of the ravines, which had been passed with great difficulty, they caught the sight of a beautiful stream on which there were three successive fine falls, each of considerable height.

Thursday, January 13.--Journey about two miles east, when they reach the summits of the table-land, at a spot not far from their former track. Here they halt on a spot covered with good grass, and well watered. Shot a kangaroo. The cattle were now so crippled, from the effects of the stoney[77] and rugged nature of the surface over which they have been travelling, during the last week in particular, that it was found necessary to cover their feet with mocassins, made of kangaroo skins, which the men had fortunately saved during the journey; and the men, for want of shoes, were not in much better condition. At three they cross Swampy Valley, a spot which they passed on the 31st of

---

avoided all those high collateral ranges, which have caused them so much distress, the last three or four days; as well as those numerous, almost insurmountable difficulties which they had to encounter afterwards.
[77] Course green granite.

October. They were now induced to diverge from their former route, hoping to find a better one, somewhat more to the eastward, when having travelled a few miles over a slightly undulating country, with but very little descent, they come to a small but rapid stream, the banks of which consisted of unsound ground, covered with a kind of rushes. Here they remain the night. The weather had been cloudy during the day, and in the evening there was a shower with thunder. The thermometer, at noon, 74 deg.

Friday, January 14.--Weather cloudy, with much lightning and thunder during the night; in the afternoon a heavy thunder squall with rain; when the weather again cleared, and became fine. The course of their route till four o'clock E N E. along the summits of the table-range; they then began to descend the eastern aspect of the range towards Limestone Valley, about six or eight miles S. of the spot at which they had ascended the range (October 29th); at six they stopped for the night, having then succeeded in effecting only about two thirds of the descent, when to their great disappointment and chagrin, the route became so craggy, dangerous and intricate, and the bullocks so exhausted, that they were utterly unable to proceed further.

Saturday, January 15.--To-day they rejoin their old track of the 28th of October, at the upper part of Limestone Valley, after a mountain journey, which for fatigue and intricacy, and even danger to the cattle, it would be impossible adequately to describe. Sometimes over steep crags, loose stones slipping from under their feet, gullies, and deep ravines traversed by small streams;--and part of the distance along the bed of a rivulet, by which they were eventually again conducted into their former track. Out of this fine little stream they had the good fortune, in the evening, to procure a few fish. The whole of their flour was expended to-day.

Sunday, January 16th.--Messrs. Hume and Hovell, with two men, hurry onwards to the carts, which they had left with part of their supplies on the 26th of October, enjoining the rest of the party to follow slowly with the bullocks, while they themselves would be occupied in conveying the carts across the stream. The carts, harness and supplies were found precisely as they had been left, except a tarpaulin, from which a piece had been cut apparently with a tomahawk, and a small spirit keg, which had leaked out, from becoming worm-eaten.--At one o'clock, the men joined with the bullocks;--when leaving two of the men to whom they were now enabled to distribute a sufficient supply of salt provisions, though without either flour or bread, in charge of the bullocks, which were at this time so exhausted, that two of them were unable to ascend the right bank of the stream, without considerable assistance;--they proceed with the horses and one of the carts, about seven miles towards the Murrumbidgee, making every possible exertion in order to procure a supply of flour, for the party whom they had left. The following day, (17th), they ford the Murrumbidgee at the same spot, at which they had before crossed it with so much difficulty. The bottom here consisted of pebbles. In the evening they rest on the banks of the Gondoroo river, at the N E. border of Yass, or M'Dougall's Plains.

On the following day (18th), they arrived in safety at Mr. Hume's station, near Lake George, from which they had taken their departure, when on their outward journey, the 17th of last October, having had the good fortune to complete in the fullest sense their arduous attempt, and to accomplish all its various objects to their utmost extent, within the short period of sixteen weeks.

From this place, they despatched the necessary supplies, for the men whom they had left behind them, on the 16th:--and on the 24th, each of them arrived at his respective home.

It now only remains to add, that after continuing a few days with the bullocks, finding them utterly unable to travel, the men left them together with what remained of the supplies, and returned in safety by themselves, following the track which had been carefully marked out for them on the trees.

The results of this important undertaking, were the discovery of a vast range of country, invaluable for every purpose of grazing, and of agriculture--watered by numerous fine streams and rivers, and presenting an easy inland intercourse, extending from Port Phillip, and Western Port, to the settled districts of Bathurst--thus refuting the previously adopted opinion, by which this same line of country, had been denounced as "uninhabitable, and useless for all the purposes of civilization,"[78] while, further, when taken in connection with the later discoveries of Captain Sturt, they give access to regions of an amplitude and capabilities fully adequate to receive, at the lowest estimate,

---

[78] For additional and more precise observations on this subject, see preface.

the entire *supposed* present surplus population of the Mother Country.

APPENDIX

No. I.

The supplies were as follow:--Seven pack saddles, one riding saddle, eight stand of arms, six pounds of gunpowder, sixty rounds of ball cartridge, six suits of slops, and six blankets for the men, two tarpaulins, one tent made of coarse Colonial woollen cloth, twelve hundred pounds of flour, three hundred and fifty pounds of pork, one hundred and seventy pounds of sugar, thirty-eight pounds of tea and coffee, eight pounds of tobacco for the men, sixteen pounds of soap, twenty pounds of salt, cooking utensils, one false horizon, one sextant, three pocket compasses, and one perambulator, exclusive of Messrs. Hovell and Hume's own personal clothes and bedding; the latter consisting, like that of the men, of a blanket only. Six of the pack saddles, the slops, and blankets for the men, with six of the muskets, and the ball-cartridges, tent, and tarpaulin, were liberally furnished by the Government; and of which, the muskets only, the other articles having become destroyed or worn out in the course of the journey, were returned.

No. II.

This note was penned and printed four years ago. Some specimens of fossil bones, which Mr. George Rankin, of Bathurst, did me the favor to shew me the other day, corroborate the justness of the suggestion. These specimens were procured from one of the limestone caves in Wellington Valley.

I have since been favored with the sight of an extensive and interesting collection, made near the same spot by Major Mitchell, Surveyor General of New South Wales.

No. III.

The Lake Alexandrina was first discovered by a boat's crew of Mr. Duncan Forbes, in the year 1829, while in command of the schooner *Prince of Denmark*; and the discovery immediately, on his arrival in Sydney, communicated by him to the Colonial Government.

No. V.

The outline of Western Port and its vicinities is given in the chart. This Port affords safe anchorage for vessels of any draft of water. The settlement lately formed by the Government, and now abandoned from the supposed desire of the Government to concentrate the powers of the Colony,--was situate on the Eastern side of the Bay. This was ill supplied, but with good water. The country from this spot to Bass River, consists principally of a rich alluvial soil; interspersed, however, here and there, with patches of heath. The amount of good land in this part of the country seemed to be about seven or eight thousand acres. The space traversed by Mr. Hovell between Bass River and Wright's River, consists almost entirely of fine land, alluvial near the Rivers, and the rest of it a good rich strong arable soil, from about 15,000 to 20,000 acres in extent. The range running between these Rivers is lofty, but not steep; fit for almost any agricultural purposes, and abounds with the best possible timber, particularly its Southern aspect. The whole of this space seemed badly watered, and the water met with, aluminous;--excepting the immediate vicinities of the Rivers which are perfectly fresh, within three or four miles of their mouths. Bass River was deep where Mr. Hovell met with it, and more than thirty feet wide. Wright's River is a somewhat smaller stream; but this was during a period of long continued drought, from which the whole Colony had most severely suffered. The space between Wright's River, Cape Patterson, and Shallow Lagoon, consists of a low undulating, heathy surface, badly watered; with here and there a patch of good timber. At Cape Patterson coal was plentiful and good, lying partly above the surface, and some of it jutting into the sea.

The space (extending from the Settlement to the Northward), to Red Buff, is a low swampy tea-tree brush, almost utterly impassable. The range immediately at the back (to the Eastward of this space) is not steep; but moderately high, abounding in timber, and almost impassable from a dense underwood.

Inland, from Red Bluff, in a Northerly direction for about 12 miles, the country consisted of open forest; with a good soil, but scantily watered; at the extremity of which distance the country became impenetrable, in consequence of the extreme *closeness* of the trees, and the denseness of the low brush and underwood. From this inland point to the entrance of Burchell River, a distance of about eight miles, the first half consisted of a dense tea-tree brush, and the remainder of excellent meadow land. Burchell River is itself a small stream, navigable for boats for not more than a quarter of a mile; but fresh down even to its entrance at low water. The country between Burchell's River and Weatherall's three inlets consisted entirely of fine open meadow land; and this, as far as it was examined, to the distance of four or five miles from the Bay. The space between the latter streams (Weatherall's inlets) and Snapper River is a low swampy impenetrable tea-tree brush.

Weatherall's inlets and Snapper River would admit craft of about 50 or 60 tons burthen, a distance of about half a mile. Both are fresh at low water. The large space extending from the entrance of Snapper River, in a Northerly direction to the Mountains; part of the Alpine Chain, a distance of about twenty miles; and again from this spot, in a Westerly direction to Port Phillip, about twenty miles, and thence to the neck of the Isthmus, as seen in the chart--a space in all of about twenty miles square, is in general an open undulating country, with here and there extensive patches of excellent meadow land, the whole of it fit for grazing, and abundantly supplied with good water.

Mr. Hovell extended his investigations of the vicinities of Western Port, until he had arrived almost on the termination of the track of the previous journey to Port Phillip, and been enabled to recognise a considerable number of the mountains and other features of the country seen on that occasion; when he was compelled to return, in consequence of the severe indisposition of two of the people, and the inadequacy of the supplies (which, from reasons not necessary to be explained here, they were compelled to carry on their persons), for a more extensive journey.

No. VI.

The opinion that the interior of this vast Island, is the site of an immense swamp, (if ever tenable) has been already refuted by the late journey to Western Port (Port Phillip) and there, therefore exists at present, at least, no confirmed opinion, relative either to the primary or the ultimate distribution of the vast bodies of water, which pursue their course into the interior regions of New Holland. These streams as far as at present known, consist of the Lachlan, the Macquarie, the Murrambidgee, the Medway, the Hume, the Ovens, and the Goulburn[79],-- seven rivers none of them inconsiderable rising among the mountains, on the Eastern Coast, pursuing their course as it appears, at present, along a considerable extent of plains, all Westerly, or North-Westerly, and the whole of them contained within the limits of 31 deg. and 37 1/2 deg. South latitude.

The opinion which Mr. Hovell begs to be allowed to offer relative to these streams is, that even should the accumulated sum total of their waters be primarily received, into one vast reservoir, that this reservoir itself, (for the waters, at least, of that portion of it discovered by the Colonial Surveyor General, should it appears be fresh) has ultimately an outlet, into the ocean; and which outlet he is induced to be of opinion from the lowness of that portion of the Coast, as well as from other circumstances connected with it, as observed by himself (but when it was not in his power to make any satisfactory examinations) will be found somewhere parallel with Lady Julia Percy's Islands. This spot is only two degrees to the westward of that portion of the Swamp, or Morass which lies due West from Sydney!!

THE END

---

[79] Now the Hovell--in order to prevent confusion--another stream having, without their knowledge at the time of their journey, been already named after the late Secretary of the Colony.

Also from Benediction Books ...
Wandering Between Two Worlds: Essays on Faith and Art
Anita Mathias
Benediction Books, 2007
152 pages
ISBN: 0955373700

Available from www.amazon.com, www.amazon.co.uk

In these wide-ranging lyrical essays, Anita Mathias writes, in lush, lovely prose, of her naughty Catholic childhood in Jamshedpur, India; her large, eccentric family in Mangalore, a sea-coast town converted by the Portuguese in the sixteenth century; her rebellion and atheism as a teenager in her Himalayan boarding school, run by German missionary nuns, St. Mary's Convent, Nainital; and her abrupt religious conversion after which she entered Mother Teresa's convent in Calcutta as a novice. Later rich, elegant essays explore the dualities of her life as a writer, mother, and Christian in the United States-- Domesticity and Art, Writing and Prayer, and the experience of being "an alien and stranger" as an immigrant in America, sensing the need for roots.

About the Author

Anita Mathias is the author of *Wandering Between Two Worlds: Essays on Faith and Art.* She has a B.A. and M.A. in English from Somerville College, Oxford University, and an M.A. in Creative Writing from the Ohio State University, USA. Anita won a National Endowment of the Arts fellowship in Creative Nonfiction in 1997. She lives in Oxford, England with her husband, Roy, and her daughters, Zoe and Irene.

Visit Anita's website
    http://www.anitamathias.com,
and Anita's blog
    http://dreamingbeneaththespires.blogspot.com, (Dreaming Beneath the Spires).

The Church That Had Too Much
Anita Mathias
Benediction Books, 2010
52 pages
ISBN: 9781849026567

Available from www.amazon.com, www.amazon.co.uk

The Church That Had Too Much was very well-intentioned. She wanted to love God, she wanted to love people, but she was both hampered by her muchness and the abundance of her possessions, and beset by ambition, power struggles and snobbery. Read about the surprising way The Church That Had Too Much began to resolve her problems in this deceptively simple and enchanting fable.

About the Author

Anita Mathias is the author of *Wandering Between Two Worlds: Essays on Faith and Art.* She has a B.A. and M.A. in English from Somerville College, Oxford University, and an M.A. in Creative Writing from the Ohio State University, USA. Anita won a National Endowment of the Arts fellowship in Creative Nonfiction in 1997. She lives in Oxford, England with her husband, Roy, and her daughters, Zoe and Irene.

Visit Anita's website
   http://www.anitamathias.com,
and Anita's blog
   http://dreamingbeneaththespires.blogspot.com (Dreaming Beneath the Spires).

www.ingramcontent.com/pod-product-compliance
Lightning Source LLC
Chambersburg PA
CBHW030519100426
42813CB00001B/86